Rashomon

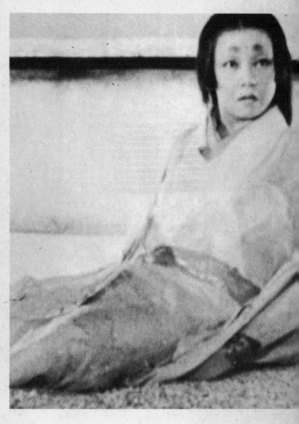

a film by Akira Kurosawa

from the filmscript by
Akira Kurosawa and Shinobu Hashimoto

Rashomon

Consulting Editor: Donald Richie
General Editor, Film Book Series: Robert Hughes

Grove Press, Inc., New York

Third Printing

ACKNOWLEDGMENTS: Frame enlargements from *Rashomon*
were made possible by the generous co-operation
of Janus Films (William Becker and Saul Turrell), the present
American distributors of the film. Most of the publicity
material for *Rashomon* was kindly provided by Daiei Motion
Picture Co. and by T. Kuroda of UniJapan Film.
  The Outrage © 1964 Metro-Goldwyn-Mayer Inc. and
KHF Productions. Excerpt of the screenplay by
Michael Kanin furnished through the courtesy of
Metro-Goldwyn-Mayer Inc., distributors of the Martin Ritt
Production *The Outrage* starring Paul Newman, Laurence
Harvey, Claire Bloom, Edward G. Robinson, William
Shatner, Howard Da Silva, Albert Salmi, produced by
A. Ronald Lubin and directed by Martin Ritt. Permission
to use the excerpt was kindly facilitated by Lewis Morton
and Mrs. Edith Tolkin of M-G-M.
  Donald Richie translated the text of *Rashomon*
from the Japanese; he also transcribed the action. The
latter was supplemented by Peter Scarlett and by
Arnold Leo. Harvey Zucker photographed the frame
enlargements, as he has for nearly all Grove film books;
Leon Levy of Film Opticals "unsqueezed" the CinemaScope
images from *The Outrage*.
  Design by Anda Pirvics.

Manufactured in the United States of America

DISTRIBUTED BY RANDOM HOUSE, INC., NEW YORK

GROVE PRESS, INC., 196 WEST HOUSTON STREET,
NEW YORK, N.Y. 10014

Contents

A Note on This Edition

When contributing editor Donald Richie once asked Akira Kurosawa about the meaning of a scene, the director replied, "If I could have said it in words, I wouldn't have gone to the trouble and expense of making a film." Paradoxically, Richie reports that with very minor exceptions the final text of *Rashomon* is almost identical to the script that Kurosawa and his long-time collaborator, Shinobu Hashimoto, had written before the filming began. Exceptions include additional shots, *e.g.*, during the woodcutter's walk through the forest and during the fights between bandit and husband; in addition, slight revisions of dialogue were made, especially in the final sequence.

The images for this book, as for *Masculine Feminine, The 400 Blows,* and *L'Avventura,* are mostly frame enlargements. Their comparative abundance in this volume is a result of our concern to render as appropriately as possible a film in which camera movement and rapid cutting play such predominant roles.

In our text, camera position is indicated by initials: LS for long shot; MS, medium shot; MCU, medium close-up; and CU, close-up. The stills keyed to the text should suggest the meaning of these terms. Camera movement is indicated by the following: *pan* (camera turning sideways while remaining fixed on its axis); *tilt* (camera moving up or down while fixed on its axis); *dolly* (camera moving toward or away from a fixed subject); *track* (camera moving at the same speed as the subject being filmed); and *travel* (camera moving at a speed independent of a moving subject). We have also noted at the end of each shot its duration in seconds. In two cases, shots last less than a second (shots 204 and 205), and these are listed in fractions.

A few points about the supplementary materials: American prints of the film, as well as all criticism we have seen with the exception of Donald Richie's, refer to the action as taking place in the ninth century; this should read twelfth century, and we have corrected such references here. Japanese and American distributors until recently have referred to the fictional basis of the film as "In a Bush" (or, alternatively, "In the Forest"), a *novel* by Akutagawa; Akutagawa's two short stories from which the film was adapted are included here. Parker Tyler's aesthetic analysis, a perceptive contemporary response to the film, is familiar to many. James Davidson's study of the social background for the creation and reception of this film in post World War II Japan seems an unjustly neglected essay, very suggestive in its insights. Curiously, exhaustive research provided no other especially relevant critical analyses of the film from either a psychological or sociological viewpoint. Donald Richie's essay on the background of the production has been extracted from his book-length study *The Films of Akira Kurosawa;* Mr. Richie, co-author with Joseph Anderson of *The Japanese Film,* also translated the principal text of *Rashomon* from the Japanese. Finally, the excerpt from M-G-M's 1964 re-make of *Rashomon,* entitled *The Outrage,* should provide interesting comparison and contrast with the original, as well as illuminating the process and problems of such adaptation.

The final page of the book reproduces the Japanese publicity poster for *Rashomon.*

—R. H.

Rashomon

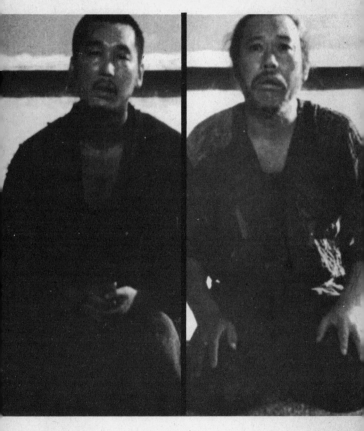

Left to right: *Tajomaru, the bandit; Masago, the wife; Take-hiro, the samurai; the woodcutter; the priest; the commoner; the medium; the police agent.*

The Film

The title sequence consists of some ten shots of the half-ruined gate, Rashomon, in the rain. Superimposed over these are the title and credits, including, in the prints distributed in the United States, vignettes (oval-shaped insets) showing the major characters in action.

Various details of the gate are seen, its steps, the base of a column, the eaves of the roof, puddles on the ground. Everywhere there is evidence of the downpour. Gagaku, traditional court music, is heard during the credits, then the sound of the torrential rain.

The final title reads: "Kyoto, in the twelfth century, when famines and civil wars had devastated the ancient capital."

1 *Long shot. Two men, a priest and a woodcutter, are sitting motionless, taking shelter under the gate.*

(4 seconds

2 *Medium shot from the side of the two, the wood-*

cutter in the foreground, as they stare out at the rain with heads bowed. The woodcutter raises his head.

WOODCUTTER: I can't understand it. I just can't understand it at all. (16

3 *Close-up of the priest; he looks at the woodcutter and back again at the rain.* (11

4 *LS from directly in front. The two men continue to stare vacantly at the rain.* (5

5 *A general view of the gate; a man enters from behind*

*the camera and runs toward the gate, splashing
through puddles. Thunder is heard.* (15

6 *LS from reverse angle. The man runs past a fallen
column, and disappears from the frame.* (2

7 *MS of the steps of the gate; he enters from behind
the camera and runs up the steps to shelter.* (4

8 *MS. Out of the rain, he turns and looks back out-*

*side, then removes a rag covering his head and wrings
it out. The woodcutter's voice is heard off-camera.*

WOODCUTTER (*off*): I just can't understand it. (11

9 *LS. The newcomer, in the background, turns toward
the priest and woodcutter, who are sitting in the
foreground.* (3

10 *MS of the newcomer. He goes toward the others—
the camera panning with him—and sits down behind
the woodcutter.*

11 *MS of the woodcutter and commoner.*

COMMONER: What can't you understand?
WOODCUTTER: I've never heard of anything so strange.
COMMONER: Why don't you tell me about it? (13

12 *MS of all three men, the priest in the foreground. The commoner looks toward the priest.*

COMMONER: Good thing we have a priest here—he looks smart too.
PRIEST: Oh, even Abbot Konin of the Kiyomizu Temple, though he's known for his learning, wouldn't be able to understand this.
COMMONER: Then you know something about this story?
PRIEST: I've heard it with my own ears, seen it with my own eyes. And only today.
COMMONER: Where?
PRIEST: In the prison courtyard.

COMMONER: The prison?
PRIEST: A man has been murdered.
COMMONER: What of it? One or two more . . . (*He stands up.*) (42

13 *MS of the commoner standing over the others; he looks down.*

COMMONER: Only one? Why, if you go up to the top of this gate you'll always find five or six bodies. Nobody bothers about them. (*He begins to take off his shirt.*) (7

14 *MS of the priest; he turns and looks up at the commoner.*

PRIEST: Oh, you're right. Wars, earthquakes, great winds, fires, famines, plague—each new year is full of disaster. (*He wipes his hand across his face.*) (19

15 (=13) *MS. The commoner wrings out his wet shirt.*
PRIEST (*off*): And now every night the bandits descend upon us. (5

16 (=14) *MS of the priest.*

PRIEST: I, for one, have seen hundreds of men dying, killed like animals. (*Pause.*) Yet . . . even I have never heard anything as horrible as this before.   *(19*

17 *MS of the woodcutter, who has been listening; he turns to the priest.*   *(3*

18 (=14) *MS. The priest turns toward the woodcutter.*   *(3*

19 *MS of the woodcutter and priest.*

WOODCUTTER: Horrible—it's horrible.

The woodcutter looks away; dolly in to CU of the priest.

PRIEST: There was never anything as terrible as this. Never. It is more horrible than fires or wars or epidemics—or bandits. (*Camera stays on him.*)

COMMONER (*off*): Look here now, priest—let's not have any sermons.

The priest looks up.   *(30*

20 (=13) *MS of the commoner.*

COMMONER: I only wanted to know about this strange story of yours because it might amuse me while I

wait out the rain. But I'd just as soon sit quietly and listen to the rain than hear any sermons from you. (*His wet shirt over his shoulder, he moves toward the camera.*) (15

21 *LS. The commoner moves away, leaving the priest and woodcutter sitting as before.* (6

22 *MS of the commoner at the other side of the gate; he peers at some loose boards, then rips two of them free.* (14

23 *LS. He crosses back to squat in front of the wood-*

cutter and priest, and begins to pull the boards to pieces. The woodcutter rises and runs over to him.

WOODCUTTER: Maybe you can tell me what it all means. I don't understand it. (*He squats down.*) All three of them . . .

COMMONER: All three of whom?

WOODCUTTER: It's those three I wanted to tell you about.

COMMONER: All right, tell me then, but don't get so excited. This rain won't let up for some time. (*Both men look up.*) (33

24 *CU of the great signboard of the gate, seen in the*

opening shot of the titles: the sign reads "Rashomon" in large Japanese characters. The camera tilts down from the signboard to the men far below. The woodcutter moves closer to the commoner.   (11

25 *CU of the woodcutter.*

WOODCUTTER: It was three days ago. I'd gone into
the mountains for wood . . .   (15

26 *The dazzling light of the sun breaks through the*

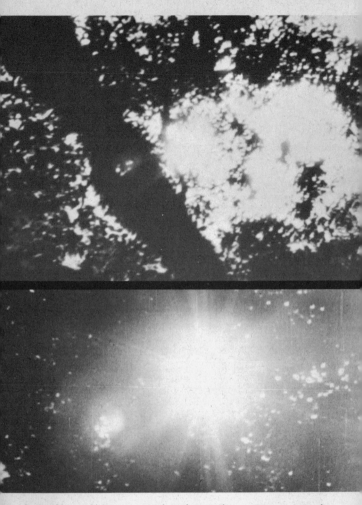

branches of trees overhead as the camera travels through a dense woods. Music begins, a steady rhythm supporting a melody initially associated with the woodcutter but later becoming the underlying musical theme of the entire film. (5

27 *CU of the woodcutter's ax, seen in a traveling shot, glinting in the sunlight as the woodcutter walks through the woods.* (7

28 *CU of the woodcutter's face as he walks, ax over his shoulder, the camera tracking backward.* (5

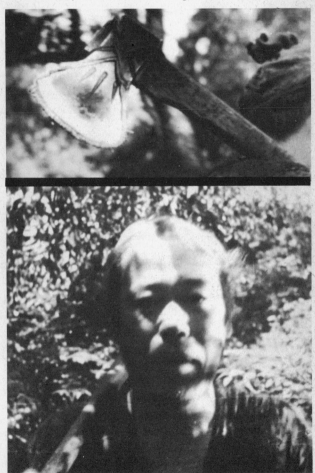

29 LS. Panning from high above, the camera follows him.   (9

30 A tree; the camera tilts from top to bottom to discover the woodcutter in the distance.   (7

31 The camera pans with the woodcutter as he approaches a narrow bridge, crosses it, and goes off. (11

32 A forward-traveling shot of the sky seen through the branches of the trees passing overhead.   (6

33 *CU of the woodcutter's back as he walks, the camera tracking after him.* (5

34 *A traveling shot as he moves from LS closer to camera.* (9

35 (=32) *The sky and the tree branches.* (6

36 *The camera travels toward the woodcutter, crosses in front of him, and pans around to follow his back receding into the woods.* (15

37 (=26) *The sun through the tree branches.* *(5*

38 *The woodcutter from above. The camera travels as the woodcutter approaches, pans, and travels with him again, closer now, occasionally losing sight of him in the underbrush.* *(15*

39 *Extreme close-up of the back of the woodcutter's head, the camera tracking after him; again, leaves sometimes block the view.* *(5*

40 *ECU. A traveling shot alongside the woodcutter; the view is frequently blocked.* *(4*

41 *ECU of the woodcutter's face as he walks, the camera tracking backward. Suddenly he halts. Music ends.* *(9*

42 CU of a woman's reed hat with veil, dangling on a branch near the ground. The woodcutter, in the background, looks at it and comes forward to touch the veil. Audible is a soft tinkle like the sound of wind chimes; it develops into a bell-like music which is later associated with the woman. The woodcutter slowly walks on, the camera panning to watch as he recedes farther into the woods. The main thematic music begins again. (25

43 MS. Traveling shot alongside the woodcutter; he

looks about on either side as he walks cautiously on. (5

44 He approaches the camera and (CU) looks down. He halts. (7

45 CU of a man's hat lying at his feet; he bends over to pick it up. The camera tilts up with him as he stands straight again. He comes forward and goes off. (11

46 LS. He approaches, stops again (MS), and looks down; this time he picks up a piece of rope, and stares in front of him. (27

47 *LS of something lying in the leaves.*   (1

48 *CU. It is an amulet case.*   (2

49 *CU of the woodcutter as he moves forward (pan)
but stumbles; he jumps back with a look of horror on
his face.*   (11

50 *MS. The stiffly raised hands of a corpse are in front
of him. A gong is sounded.*   (2

51 *CU of the woodcutter's face; he leaps back, turns
around and, his back to the camera, runs into the
woods, dropping his ax as he goes.*   (7

52 *MS. The camera moves rapidly alongside the woodcutter as he runs panic-stricken through the woods.
His speech runs over this and the next two shots.*
WOODCUTTER *(off)*: I ran as fast as I could to tell the
   police. That was three days ago. Then the police
   called me to testify.   (3

53 *MS. The camera continues to move with the woodcutter.*   (3

54 *MS. The camera continues with him. (Wipe.)*   (3

55 *MS of the woodcutter kneeling on the sand of the
prison courtyard.*
WOODCUTTER: Yes, sir. It was I who found the body
   first. (*Pause. He is obviously being questioned though
   we hear only his answers.*) Was there a sword or
   anything? No, sir. Nothing at all. Only a woman's hat,
   caught on a branch . . . and a man's hat that had

been trampled on. And a piece of rope . . . and further off an amulet case of red brocade. (*Pause.*) Yes, sir. Yes, that was all I saw. I swear it. (*He bows.*) (*Wipe.*) (52

56 *MS of the priest kneeling in the prison courtyard.*
Behind him is the woodcutter. The priest is testifying.

PRIEST: Yes, sir, I saw the murdered man when he
was still alive. Well, it was about three days ago. It

was in the afternoon. Yes. It was on the road between Sekiyama and Yamashina. *(23*

57 *The priest is walking along a road which winds through a bamboo grove. Music in. Pan as he approaches the camera and passes it. He stops. From the opposite direction a samurai approaches, leading a horse by the bridle. On the horse is a woman, sitting*

34

sidesaddle. The priest steps back and looks after them (pan) as they recede into the distance.

PRIEST (*off*): Her hat had a veil. I couldn't see her face. The man was armed. He had a sword, bow and arrows. (*A gong sounds.*) (35

58 (=56) *MS of the priest in the prison courtyard.*

PRIEST: I never thought I would see him again; then, to

see him dead like that. Oh, it is true—life is ephemeral, as fleeting as the morning dew. But the pity of it. What a pity that he should have died like that. (*He bows.*) (*Wipe.*) (29

59 *MS. The police agent is proudly testifying. Beside him, tied up, sits the bandit, Tajomaru. Behind them sit the woodcutter and the priest.*

POLICE AGENT: Yes, it was I who caught Tajomaru. Yes, indeed. That very same notorious bandit who has been so much talked about, even in the outskirts of the city. (10

60 *CU of the bandit gazing vacantly up at the sky, the voice of the agent continuing.* (2

61 *The sky, filled with huge summer clouds.*

POLICE AGENT (*continuing, off*): Yes, this is the very same bandit, Tajomaru, your honor. When I finally caught him . . . (2

62 (=59) *MS of the agent testifying.*

POLICE AGENT: . . . he was dressed like he is now, and carried that Korean sword. It was toward evening, day before yesterday, by the riverbank at Katsura. (*Dolly to CU of agent.*) (16

63 *The riverbank. Music in. The agent walks toward the camera, hears a horse neigh, and runs (pan) along the bank toward a man lying as though in agony (LS). He leans over to lift the man and loses his grip, stumbling back into the river.* (21

64 *MS. Tajomaru, in the foreground, groaning, ap-parently in agony, writhing in the sand. In the back-ground, the agent in the river. The camera travels from them to reveal, farther down the bank, a bow, arrows, a horse.*

POLICE AGENT (*off*): There was a black-lacquered quiver holding seventeen arrows in all—they all had hawk feathers. The bow was bound in leather . . . and there was a gray horse.   (19

65 *CU of the agent in the prison courtyard; the camera backs away from CU of him to same position as shot 59.*

POLICE AGENT: And they all belonged to the murdered man. But just imagine a fierce bandit like Tajomaru here being thrown by the very animal that he him-self had stolen. It was retribution.

The bandit wheels toward him threateningly, hisses through his teeth, then bursts into laughter.

TAJOMARU: Retribution? Don't be stupid. On that day . . .   (34

66 *LS. A hill, low clouds. Triumphant music. Tajomaru, shouting, gallops across and off the screen.*

TAJOMARU (*continuing, off*): . . . while I was riding that gray horse I suddenly got very thirsty. *(9*

67 *MS of Tajomaru, continuing in the prison courtyard.*

TAJOMARU: So when I got near Osaka Pass I had a
    drink at a stream.   (7

68 *LS from above. Tajomaru, stretched on the ground, drinks from a small stream. His heavy panting is heard.*
(13

69 (=67) *MS of Tajomaru in the prison courtyard.*

TAJOMARU: There must have been a snake or something in the upper stream, because after a few hours I began to have this terrible colic. Toward evening it got so I couldn't bear it any longer and so I got off the horse and lay down. (*Dolly back to the two-shot [59] of Tajomaru and the police agent.*) And you thought I'd fallen off—hah! (*He hisses and kicks the quiver lying in front of the agent.*) It takes a pretty stupid person to have an idea that stupid.
(29

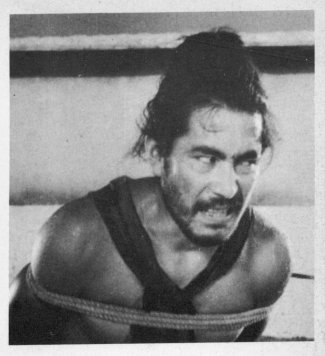

70 *CU of Tajomaru.*

TAJOMARU: No, I'm telling the truth. I know you're going to cut off my head sooner or later—I'm not hiding anything. It was me, Tajomaru, who killed that man. Yes, I did it. It was a hot afternoon, about three days ago, that I first saw them. And then all of a sudden there was this cool breeze. If it hadn't been for that breeze, maybe I wouldn't have killed him.

The bell-like music, like distant wind chimes, is heard as he concludes; the tinkling continues into the next shot. (32

71 *In the woods; the camera tilts from the great crown*

of an enormous tree down to its roots to reveal the bandit sprawled out sleeping at the base of another huge tree nearby. Music denoting the traveling couple fades in over the tinkling bells. (10

72 MS of Tajomaru asleep; the camera dollies in to CU of him and pans around to reveal the samurai leading the horse on which the woman is riding. (20

73 *Back-traveling shot of the pair coming down the road.* (3

74 *CU of the bandit; he looks sleepily in their direction.* (3

75 *CU of the woman on horseback, her face barely visible through the veil of her hat.* (3

76 *(=74) CU. Tajomaru closes his eyes, scratches, appears to be falling asleep again, but suddenly glances in the direction of the couple.* (19

77 *LS. The pair approach the "sleeping" figure.* (6

78 *MS profile of the samurai as he sees Tajomaru and hesitates.* (2

79 *(=74) CU. Tajomaru, his eyes half-open, staring back at the samurai.* (4

80 *MS. The samurai, now seen from in front, continues to assess Tajomaru.* (3

81 *(=74) CU. Tajomaru staring back; he scratches his leg lazily, closing his eyes again.* (11

82 *CU. The samurai decides to move on, leading the horse toward the camera.* (5

83 *(=74) CU of Tajomaru, his eyes shut. Then, to the sound of the bell-like music, a fresh breeze stirs his hair; he opens his eyes, looks in the couple's direction, and gives a start.* (13

84 *CU of the feet of the woman, gently swinging with the movements of the horse; the camera tilts up to show her face as the veil is blown aside.* (3

85 *ECU of Tajomaru, now wide-awake, looking.* (3

86 *CU of the woman on horseback (pan), her veil part-ing to reveal her face fully.* (3

87 *(=85) ECU. Tajomaru raises himself up.* (4

88 *MS from behind Tajomaru, now in a sitting position. Pan as the horse and couple move past him in the background. Tajomaru turns and looks after them, then sinks back under the tree as they continue to move farther down the road.* (25

89 *MS of Tajomaru, from in front. His sword rests be-*
tween his legs, and now he slowly pulls it closer to him.
(12

90 (=70) *In the prison courtyard, Tajomaru continues*
his testimony.

TAJOMARU: It was just a glimpse. First I saw her, then
she was gone—I thought I had seen an angel. And
right then I decided I would take her, that I'd have
her even if I had to kill the man. . . . (*He laughs.*)
But if I could do it without killing him, then that
would be all the better. So I decided not to kill
him but to somehow get the woman alone. The
road to Yamashina was hardly the place to do it
though.
(35

91 *LS. Tajomaru runs through the woods toward the camera. Chase music in.* (3

92 *LS from the side; the camera travels with him as he races along.* (2

93 *MS. He runs down a slope (pan).* (3

94 *MS. Pan to follow him as he leaps over a small brook and approaches the couple in the background. Music out.* (4

95 *MS of Tajomaru's back, the couple visible over his shoulder. The samurai stops and turns.*
SAMURAI: What do you want? (3

96 *CU of Tajomaru's face. He stares back at the samurai, absently slaps at a mosquito that has landed on his neck, then walks (pan) behind the horse (MS), glancing up at the woman.* (15

97 *CU as Tajomaru eyes the pair, then walks to the front of horse (MS) and crouches down.*

SAMURAI (*off*): What is it? (11

98 *MS from behind the samurai as he approaches Tajomaru.*

SAMURAI (*threateningly*): What do you want?

Tajomaru rises and crosses back behind the horse (pan), into a clearing. As the samurai crosses in front of the horse into the clearing, Tajomaru suddenly draws his sword and swings it smartly—the samurai at once reaches for his own sword, but the bandit laughs loudly, for he is merely displaying his. (26

MS. Reverse angle from behind Tajomaru's back as he proudly raises his sword.

TAJOMARU: Isn't that splendid? Just look! (5

100 *MS of Tajomaru as he steps up to the samurai and presents the sword, hilt first.*

TAJOMARU: Here, take it. Look at it. (*The samurai makes no move to accept it.*) Near here I found this old tomb (*points past camera*) with lots of things like

this in it. I broke it open and inside found swords, daggers, mirrors. . . . I buried them all here in the woods and no one but me knows where. But if you're interested I might sell some of them to you cheap. (*Presents the sword again.*)   (30

101 *CU from reverse angle as Tajomaru holds out the sword. The samurai abruptly takes it and examines it. Tajomaru glances in the woman's direction and*

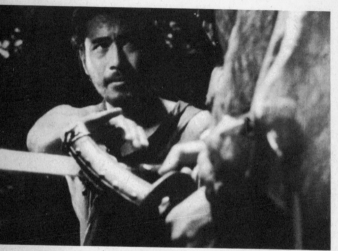

scratches his cheek. (Wipe.)   (16

102 *The forest, enormous trees. Idyllic music. The camera tilts down to reveal the woman sitting on the ground alone, the horse grazing behind her.*   (25

103 *CU of the bow and arrows, which have been left lying on the ground near the woman.*   (3

104 *LS. The bandit and the samurai are climbing a slope in the woods; a traveling shot from above and*

behind them. *Music with drums accompanies the trek through the woods.* (13

105 *MS from above and in front of them as they continue up the slope (pan).* (9

106 *LS. They push on through the woods (pan).* (9

107 *MS. Pan as they go on. Suddenly Tajomaru stops and draws his sword. The man recoils, thinking the*

bandit is about to fight. Tajomaru laughs and with a shout pokes his sword toward the samurai. Then he begins slashing at the obstructing underbrush with the sword (pan). (13

108 *CU. Pan as the bandit hacks his way forward. He pauses.*

TAJOMARU: It's over there in that grove. (11

109 *CU of the samurai, eyeing the bandit.*

SAMURAI: You walk ahead of me. (4

110 *MS. Tajomaru, in the background, waits, then turns from the camera and starts out, leading the way for the samurai.*
(10

111 *MS. Tajomaru, hacking through the underbrush, leads the way as the two come toward the camera, which tracks backward.*
(7

112 *MS. Now the camera tracks forward and follows their backs.*
(6

113 *MS. They approach the camera; it pans as they go off.*
(14

114 *MS. They approach from LS. Tajomaru stops and gestures.*

TAJOMARU: It's over there. (*He replaces his sword in its scabbard.*)

The samurai moves past and in front of him (pan), and stands looking with his back to Tajomaru.
(23

115 *CU of Tajomaru—pan as he attacks the other man, knocking him to the ground. Fight music punctuates the action. They roll over each other, but Tajomaru kicks the samurai away, then leaps through the air after him. The remainder of the fight is never seen, for as Tajomaru leaps, a wipe leads into shot 116.* (18

116 *MS. A traveling shot of Tajomaru running through the woods. He pauses for a moment to point back in the direction of the samurai, laughing and shouting.* (7

117 *CU. The camera continues to travel with him.* (4

118 *LS. Still running and laughing loudly, he starts down a hill.* (7

119 *LS from the bottom of the hill. Tajomaru descends, stops, and peers through the bushes (CU).* (25

120 *Over his shoulder, far below, stands the woman, waiting by a small brook. She crouches to dangle her hand in the water.* (12

121 *MS. A closer view of the waiting woman.* (4

122 (=119) *CU. Tajomaru looks down at her, his eyes wide.* (4

123 *CU of the woman, serenely passing the time.* (3

124 (=119) *CU. Tajomaru peering down.* (2

125 *ECU of the woman's hand, playing with the water*

as it flows gently past. Suddenly her hand stops. *(5*

126 *CU of the woman from the side as she turns abruptly to the camera, puzzled, and lifts her veil. (3*

127 *(=119) CU. Tajomaru sees she has noticed something and leaps forward from his hiding place. (3*

128 *CU from reverse angle. Tajomaru's back as he bounds down toward her away from the camera. (6*

129 *MS. Reverse angle from over the woman's shoulder. Tajomaru runs swiftly up to her and stops, panting, in front of her.*

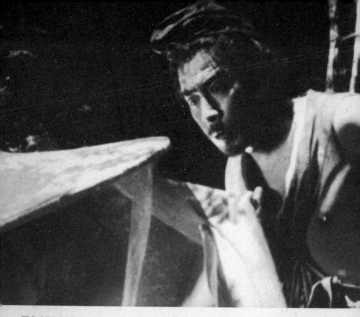

TAJOMARU: Something terrible has happened. Your
husband's been bitten by a snake. (5

130 *MS. Reverse angle of the woman from behind
Tajomaru. Shocked, she stands up, removing her hat.*
(3

131 *CU of the bareheaded woman; she stares in-
credulously at the bandit.* (4

132 *CU of Tajomaru in the prison courtyard, continuing his testimony.*

TAJOMARU: She became very pale and stared at me as
though her eyes were frozen. She looked like a
child when it turns suddenly serious. The sight of her
made me jealous of that man; I started to hate him.
I wanted to show her what he looked like, all tied
up like that. I hadn't even thought of a thing like
that before, but now I did. (29

59

133 *MS. A traveling shot of Tajomaru running through the woods, pulling the woman after him. Travel music begins.* (5

134 *MS of the woman; a traveling shot as she is pulled along by the wrist.* (3

135 *CU. A traveling shot of her hat dragging behind her; it snags on a branch (camera stops) and is left behind.* (7

136 *They run from LS up to the camera, which pans to reveal the samurai, tightly bound up, sitting in the clearing where Tajomaru attacked him. The woman stops abruptly.* (5

137 *CU of the samurai, helpless.* (1

138 *CU. The woman stands transfixed by the sight of her husband, Tajomaru behind her; the bandit steps forward past her.* (7

139 *LS from behind the husband, the woman and Tajomaru in the background: Tajomaru steps back to look at both of them.* (9

140 *MS from behind the husband, the woman in the background.* (4

141 *MS from behind the bandit, the husband in the background.* (3

142 *MS from the side of the woman, the bandit in the background.* (4

143 *MS from the side of the bandit, the woman in the background.*   (5

144 *MS from behind the husband, the bandit in the background. The samurai looks toward his wife.*   (6

145 *MS from the side of the woman, her husband in the background. The camera moves swiftly toward her and*

pans around her (CU) as she suddenly turns to attack the bandit with her dagger. She races toward him, her weapon outstretched, but he dodges the thrust and springs around to look at her with admiring disbelief.
(18

146 CU of her frenzied face as she regains her balance and whirls to charge again. (3

147 MS from behind her as she runs at him again

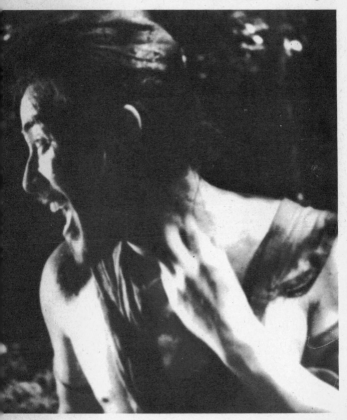

(pan); he dodges, she turns and charges at him with the dagger held straight before her. Hysterical now, she misses and stumbles out of sight. The camera remains on Tajomaru's laughing face. (5

148 MS. Tajomaru in the foreground, the woman in the background; she dives forward and grabs his leg, but he pulls free. (4

149 *CU of Tajomaru; he stares down at her, excited by her desperate spirit.* (3

150 *CU of the woman, stretched on the ground; she menaces him with the dagger held straight up at him, every muscle tense and ready.* (3

151 (=149) *CU. Tajomaru's admiration is unbounded.*
(3

152 (=150) *CU. She won't relent.*

TAJOMARU (*off*): She was fierce, determined . . .   (5

153 *MS of the two of them; he continues to stand over her, silent, watchful.*

TAJOMARU (*off*): She fought like a cat.

She rises, slashes at him. (14

154 *MS from reverse angle as he grabs her.* (4

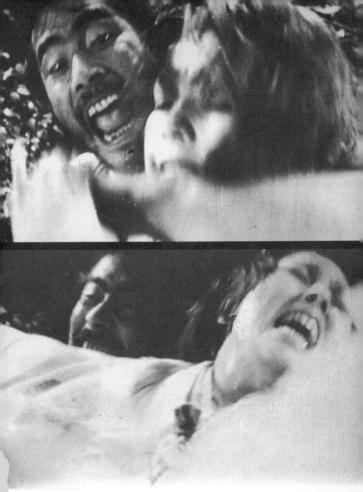

155 *CU. He shouts in pain as she sinks her teeth into his forearm; he flings her away and (pan) she trips to the ground.* (4

156 *CU of Tajomaru; he licks his wound and moves forward.* (9

157 *CU of the woman as she rises to attack again.* (2

158 *LS. She chases him, wildly slicing the air with her dagger (pan). He circles round a tree and continues in the opposite direction (pan).* (6

159 *MS from left. He reaches another tree, swings around it, and waits for her next move. She thrusts at him, sobbing, and they chase each other around the tree.* (16

160 *MS from right. He runs off (traveling shot); she follows, but collapses, exhausted; he stands jubilant over her.* (12

161 *LS. The woman in the foreground, helplessly sobbing; Tajomaru in the background. He stalks up to her, she lunges yet again, but now he grabs and holds her.* (15

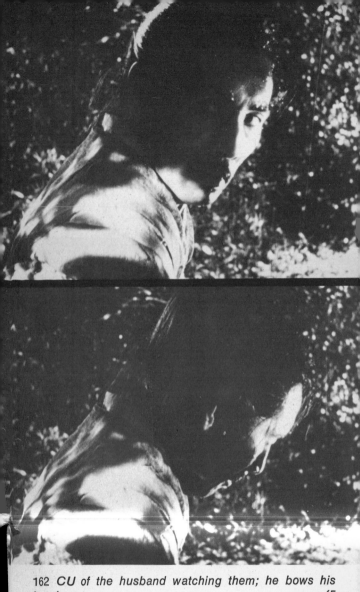

162 *CU of the husband watching them; he bows his head.* (5

163 *CU. The woman claws Tajomaru's face; he wrests his head free and pushes her to the ground (camera*

tilts down). She struggles but he kisses her. (7

164 *The sky seen through the branches of the trees (pan).* (2

165 *CU of the bandit kissing her; she stares straight up.* (4

166 (=164) *The sky seen through the overhead branches (pan).* (2

167 *CU from reverse angle; Tajomaru holding her, kissing her.* (1

168 (=164) *The sky and trees. The camera has stopped panning; now the sun is seen shining brilliantly through the branches. Bell-like music begins.* (3

169 *ECU from reverse angle; Tajomaru kissing the woman, as she stares blankly up at the sun.* (3

170 (=168) *The sun through the branches; slowly the scene goes out of focus.* (4

171 (=169) *ECU. The woman closes her eyes.* (4

172 *ECU of the dagger in her hand, Tajomaru tightly*

gripping her wrist. Her fingers loosen, the dagger drops
to the ground. (3

173 *ECU of the dagger sticking point first in the*
ground. (2

174 *MS of Tajomaru's back, the woman in his arms. The camera slowly dollies toward them. Her hand encircles his back, her fingers move caressingly; she tightens her grip on him. She is giving herself.* (11

175 *MS. In the prison courtyard, Tajomaru is laughing and kicking his feet exultantly.*

TAJOMARU: And so I had her—just as I'd planned, and without killing the husband. And that was how I did it. Besides, I hadn't intended to kill him. But then . . . *(21*

176 *CU of Tajomaru's back as he walks away from the camera to go off into the woods; the woman rushes after him (LS).* *(4*

177 *MS from reverse angle. She throws herself at his feet.*

WOMAN: Wait. Stop. One of you must die. Either you or my husband. *(13*

178 *CU of her husband. Bound up, he stares without expression.* *(3*

179 *CU of Tajomaru staring at the samurai; then he looks down at the woman.* *(3*

180 *CU of the woman kneeling, seen from over Tajomaru's shoulder.*

WOMAN: Either you or he must die. To be doubly disgraced, disgraced before two men, is more than I can bear. (7

181 *CU of Tajomaru looking down at her.* (2

182 *(=180) CU. The woman continues to speak intensely.*

WOMAN: I want . . . I will belong to whoever kills the other. (10

183 *ECU of the woman; her honor at stake, she looks up expectantly at the bandit.* (5

184 *ECU of Tajomaru. A fierce resolution comes over his face.* (5

185 *CU of the woman on the ground. Tajomaru walks away to the samurai in the background (LS). The woman remains in the foreground with lowered eyes. Tajomaru takes out his sword.* (11

186 *MS. Tajomaru cuts the ropes binding the samurai, and holds out the unsheathed sword he has robbed from him. The samurai whips the sword from its scabbard and slashes at Tajomaru. The samurai then springs to his feet and they begin to fight (pan). They move away from the camera into the background.* (18

187 *MS. The two duel, slashing and parrying. Martial music.* (9

188 *CU. Tajomaru turns, thrusts at the samurai.* (1

189 *CU of Tajomaru's sword as the samurai dodges; Tajomaru pulls back and they cross swords again.* (2

190 *MS. The two of them fighting, Tajomaru in the foreground; the bandit heads away from the camera and scrambles up a slight incline.* (8

191 *MS. He slips and falls, but remains there in a sitting position, glaring defiantly at his opponent.* (7

192 *MS from reverse angle. The bandit's back in the foreground, the samurai visible below. Tajomaru scratches idly, then charges down the incline past the other man. Now in the background, the bandit turns and starts to walk insouciantly away, then whirls on his opponent.* (13

193 *Tajomaru lunges forward, the samurai backs out of the frame, Tajomaru follows. The samurai charges back into the frame, followed again by the bandit. They fight toward the background; the samurai stumbles.* (7

194 *CU. The samurai, stumbling, falls to a sitting position.* (1

195 *MS. Tajomaru, in the background, circles menacingly around the samurai in the foreground.* (11

196 (=194) *CU of the samurai on guard, ready to ward off Tajomaru's attack.* (3

197 *CU of the bandit jabbing at the fallen samurai.* (2

198 (=194) *CU of the samurai warding off the thrust.* (2

199 (=197) *CU of the bandit circling (pan), brandishing his sword, sometimes feinting a lunge.* (8

200 (=194) *The samurai, still in a sitting position, turns with Tajomaru.* (1

201 (=197) *CU of the bandit circling (pan) in the other direction.* (1

202 (=194) *CU of the samurai, still sitting, sword in a defensive position.* (4

203 (=197) *CU of the bandit (pan) taunting, feinting— finally he lunges.* (10

204 *ECU. The samurai, who has kept in his free hand the rope that had bound him, now whips the rope at Tajomaru.* (½

205 (=197) *CU. The bandit wards off the rope.* (½

206 *MS. The samurai is on his feet again, and the two cross swords, circling around so that the samurai's back is to the camera.* (4

207 *MS from reverse angle. The two men fight, running, struggling; they begin to duel around a tree, Tajomaru pursuing.* (5

208 *Camera dollies in to ECU of the two men fighting around the tree.* (7

209 *LS through the bushes of a thicket. The samurai is forced back into the thicket, his back to the camera; then he stumbles and falls on his back. Tajomaru moves in on him. The samurai's sword has become entangled in the undergrowth. Dolly in to MS of Tajomaru, who laughs, raises his sword to throw it, and spears the samurai with a mighty heave. Tajomaru stands looking down.* (27

210 *MS. In the prison courtyard, Tajomaru continues.*
TAJOMARU: I wanted to kill him honestly, since I had

to kill him. And he fought really well. We crossed swords over twenty-three times. Think of that! No one had ever crossed over twenty with me before. Then I killed him. (*He laughs.*)

The camera has dollied back to reveal the police agent, as well as the priest and the woodcutter in the background.

TAJOMARU (*answering the unheard voice of the official questioner*): What's that? The woman? Oh, she wasn't around anywhere. Probably got frightened and ran away. She must have been really upset. Anyway, when I came down the path again I found the horse grazing there. About that woman—it was her temper that interested me, but she turned out to be just like any other woman. I didn't even look for her. (*Pause.*) What? His sword? Oh, I sold that in town on the same day, then drank the money up. (*Pause.*) Her dagger? I remember, it looked valuable, had some kind of inlay in it. You know what I did? I forgot all about it. What a fool thing to do. Walked off and forgot it. That was the biggest mistake I ever made. (*Laughs uproariously, kicking his feet on the ground.*)

(97

211 *CU of the rain pouring off the eaves of the Rash-omon; the sound of the great downpour. Tilt down to reveal the three men below.* (14

212 *MS of the woodcutter, in the foreground, and the*

commoner, sitting by a fire; the commoner stretches and yawns.

COMMONER: Oh, that Tajomaru, he's famous for that sort of thing. He's worse than all the other bandits in Kyoto. Why, last fall a young girl went off with her maid to worship at the Toribe Temple and they found them murdered there afterwards. He must have done it. (*He rises to fetch some wood.*)　　　　(31

213 *LS. The priest in the foreground; the commoner, in the background, continues talking as he crosses behind the priest.*

COMMONER: They say the woman ran away and left her horse behind. I just bet he killed her.

He pulls some loose planks from the side of the gate. The priest rises to walk back to the commoner.

PRIEST: But the woman turned up in prison too, you know.

The commoner turns to listen.　　　　(19

214 *MS from reverse angle, commoner in the foreground. The priest approaches the commoner.*

PRIEST: It seems she went to seek refuge at some temple and the police found her there.

The voice of the woodcutter cuts across this.

WOODCUTTER (*off*): It's a lie!　　　　(8

215 *CU of the woodcutter, the priest and commoner visible in the background.*

WOODCUTTER: It's a lie. They're all lies! Tajomaru's confession, the woman's story—they're lies!

COMMONER: Well, men are only men. That's why they lie. (*He pulls a board loose and turns to speak again.*) They can't tell the truth, not even to themselves.

PRIEST: That may be true. But it's because men are so weak. That's why they lie. That's why they must deceive themselves.

COMMONER: Not another sermon! (*He starts to move forward.*) (34

216 *MS of the commoner, leaning forward as he puts the wood on the fire.*

COMMONER: I don't mind a lie. Not if it's interesting. What kind of story did she tell? (*He looks up.*) (11

217 *MS of the priest.*

PRIEST: Hers was a completely different story from the bandit's. (*He comes up and kneels between the others, the camera panning with him.*) Everything was different. (10

218 *CU of the priest.*

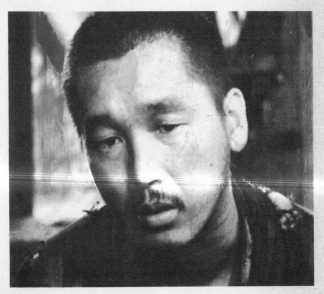

PRIEST: Tajomaru talked about her temper, her strength. I saw nothing like that at all. I found her very pitiful. I felt great compassion for her. *(20*

219 *LS of the woman in the prison courtyard, the woodcutter and priest in the background. The main thematic music begins softly and continues, almost uninterrupted, throughout the woman's version of the story. At times gentle, at other times frenzied, it is the*

only musical theme through shot 254. The woman is bent over weeping; she raises her head.   (13

220 *MS of the woman.*

WOMAN: And then, after having taken advantage of me, he told me—oh, so proudly—that he was the famous bandit Tajomaru. And then he sneered at my husband.   (38

221 *CU as she continues, now more possessed.*

WOMAN: Oh, how terrible it must have been for him. But the more he struggled, the tighter the ropes became. I couldn't stand it. Not even realizing what I was doing, I ran toward him, or tried to.   (42

222 *LS. The woods. With her back to the camera, the woman runs toward her husband; the bandit pushes past her, knocking her down, and goes up to the husband bound by the tree. He takes the husband's sword and starts to leave.*   (10

223 *MS of Tajomaru as he turns to sneer at the husband. The woman's sobs are heard and Tajomaru begins to laugh and point at the husband, then turns away.*   (7

224 *LS as Tajomaru stops to laugh again, jumping up and down; then he runs off, disappearing into the woods.*   (11

225 *LS. The woman lies weeping on the ground by her husband.*   (7

226 *LS. The same, from nearer.*   (5

227 *MS. The same, nearer still.*   (7

228 *CU of the woman, sobbing; finally she raises her head to look brokenheartedly at her husband.*   (19

229 *CU of her husband, in profile. He stares at the ground.* (3

230 (=228) *CU. She looks at him, then begins to rise.* (7

231 *LS from behind the woman as she rushes toward her husband in the background and throws herself on him.* (5

232 *CU from over his shoulder. She sobs on his breast, looks up, and is shocked by what she sees. (21*

233 *CU of the husband from over her shoulder. He looks at her coldly, cynically.* (3

234 *MS. In the prison courtyard, the woman continues, the woodcutter and priest visible in the background.*

WOMAN: Even now I remember his eyes. . . . What I saw in them was not sorrow, not even anger. It was . . . a cold hatred of me. *(36*

235 *MS in the woods, the woman seen over her husband's shoulder. She pulls herself away from him, staring at him. As she speaks, she moves from side to side before him, the camera moving with her.*

WOMAN: Don't look at me like that. Don't! Beat me, kill me if you must, but don't look at me like that. Please don't! *(43*

236 *CU. She covers her face with her hands and starts to sink back to the ground.* *(16*

237 *ECU of the top of her head as she lies shaking and sobbing.* *(32*

238 *CU. Suddenly she looks up, glances around, starts to rise.* (4

239 *LS. The pair in the background; in the foreground is the dagger, still sticking point first in the ground. She rises to her feet, comes forward and retrieves it, and rushes back to her husband, starting to cut his bonds.* (13

240 *CU. The dagger cutting through the rope.* (1

241 *MS over the husband's shoulder; she extends the dagger to him.*

WOMAN: Then kill me if you will. Kill me with one stroke—quickly!

The camera dollies toward her face, then pans around to show the husband still staring at her as before.   (29

242 *CU. She looks up imploringly, rises, and starts to back away.*   (9

243 *MS. The camera dollies with her as she backs away.*
WOMAN: Oh, don't! Please don't!
She raises her hands to her face, still clutching the dagger.   (9

---

244 *CU of the husband's hard, unmoved face.*
WOMAN (*off*): Don't—don't look at me like that!   (1

245 *CU. She comes forward again, dagger extended.*
WOMAN: Don't.   (7

246 (=244) *CU of the husband staring; her sobs are heard.*   (1

247 (=245) *CU of the woman, backing off again, crying.*
                                                      (3

248 (=244) *CU of the husband, as before.*   (1

249 (=245) *CU. She continues to move, the camera seeming to weave with her painful approach and retreat before her husband. She holds the dagger almost absent-mindedly; her desperation grows.*   (7

250 (=244) *CU of the husband, staring implacably.* (1

251 *CU of the woman as she moves steadily forward now; her world forever destroyed, she holds the dagger*

*high, without seeming to be aware of it. The camera
tracks with her in the direction of her husband until
she suddenly lunges off screen.* (21

252 (=234) *MS of the woman in the prison courtyard,
continuing her testimony.*

WOMAN: And then I fainted. When I opened my eyes
and looked around, I saw there, in my husband's
chest, the dagger. (*She begins to weep again.*) I
didn't know what to do. I ran through the forest—I
must have, although I don't remember. Then I found
myself standing by a pond . . . (105

253 *Shot of a lake, illuminated by a low sun, a strong
breeze moving over the surface.*

WOMAN (*continuing, off*): . . . at the foot of a hill. (5

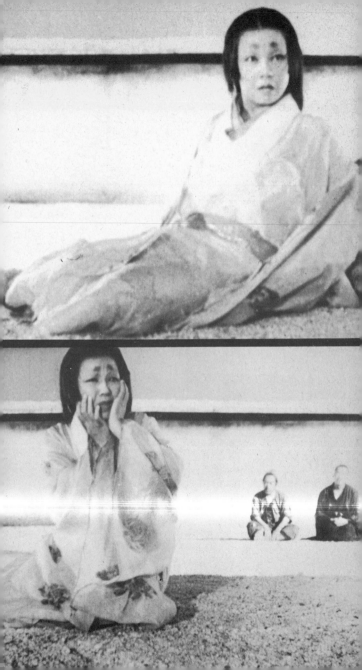

254 (=234) *MS of the woman in the prison courtyard.*

WOMAN: I threw myself into it. I tried to kill myself. But, I failed. (*She sobs.*) What should a poor helpless woman like me do? (*She sinks to the ground.*)   (50

255 *CU of the steps of the Rashomon with the rain
pouring down. The dreary, loud sound of the rain.
Visible above the steps are the three men, seated. The
camera tilts up as the commoner stands; he comes*

forward, looks out at the sky, spits disgustedly, and
turns back to the group. (23

256 *MS. He rejoins the other two around the fire (pan).*

COMMONER: I see. But the more I listen the more
  mixed up I get. (*He sits down.*) Women lead you on
  with their tears; they even fool themselves. Now if I
  believed what she said I'd really be mixed up.
PRIEST: But according to the husband's story . . .
COMMONER: But he's dead. How could a dead man
  talk?
PRIEST: He spoke through a medium.
WOODCUTTER: Lies. (*He rises and comes toward the
  camera.*) His story was all lies.
PRIEST: Dead men tell no lies. (46

257 *CU of the commoner, in the foreground, and the
priest.*

COMMONER: All right, priest—why is that?

PRIEST: They must not. I must not believe that men are so sinful. (7

258 *CU of the two from reverse angle.*

COMMONER: Oh, I don't object to that. After all, who's honest nowadays? Look, everyone wants to forget unpleasant things, so they make up stories. It's easier that way. (*Grinning, he bites into a piece of fruit. The priest looks distraught.*) But never mind. Let's hear this dead man's story. (31

259 *The ceiling and beams of the great gate illuminated by a tremendous flash of lightning.* (1

260 *LS from above the three men as they look up. A roll of thunder is heard.* (3

261 *MS of a fallen statue outside the gate. The rain falls even harder, flooding in rapid cascades past the statue.* (3

262 CU of the statue. (2

263 *CU of a hand bell being violently shaken in the air. The scene has abruptly shifted back to the prison courtyard.* (1

264 *MS of the medium, a woman, her hair and robes*

blowing in the wind. She is rattling the bell, dancing madly. The bell clatters, the wind howls, and a weird, unearthly voice drones on like a record player slowing down. A drum beats slowly. The wind, voice, and drum continue through shot 273.　　　　　　　　　　*(3*

265 *LS from above the medium. Behind her kneel the woodcutter and the priest. She circles the altar which has been placed in the courtyard, shaking the bell. (6*

266 (=263) *CU of the bell being shaken.*　　　　　　*(1*

267 *MS of the medium writhing about on her feet. She begins to turn dizzily in circles. Suddenly she stops completely still.*　　　　　　　　　　　　　　　*(11*

268 *CU of the medium, now possessed by the other world.*　　　　　　　　　　　　　　　　　　　*(3*

269 *CU of the bell dropping from her hand.*　　　　*(1*

270 (=268) *CU. She turns abruptly to face the camera.*
　　　　　　　　　　　　　　　　　　　　　　(1

271 *LS. She rushes toward the foreground and stands, mouth open, her eyes wild, as the camera dollies in. Her mouth begins to move and suddenly the voice of the dead man is heard.*

SAMURAI-MEDIUM (*as though at a great distance*): I am in darkness now. I am suffering in the darkness. Cursed be those who cast me into this hell of darkness. (*The medium starts to fall.*) *(27*

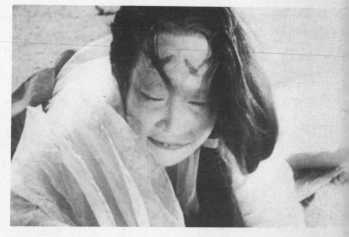

272 *MS of the medium falling behind the altar to the ground. She moves convulsively on the ground, the camera panning with her.* *(15*

273 *MS. She sits upright as the camera dollies in to an ECU. Her mouth opens and over the sound of the wind the voice of the samurai is heard.*

SAMURAI-MEDIUM: The bandit, after attacking my wife, sat down beside her and tried to console her. (*The sound of the unearthly voice and drum stops abruptly.*) *(27*

274 *LS. The woods. In the clearing where the rape*

*took place, the bandit is sitting beside the woman,
talking to her, touching her arm to get her attention.
The samurai's story is accompanied by a somber
musical theme which plays over most of the scenes
through shot 305.*

SAMURAI-MEDIUM (*off*): She sat there on the leaves,
looking down, looking at nothing. The bandit was
cunning.

*Camera dollies back to reveal the husband bound in
the foreground.*

SAMURAI-MEDIUM (*off*): He told her that after she had
given herself, she would no longer be able to live
with her husband—why didn't she go with him, the
bandit, rather than remain behind to be unhappy

with her husband? He said he had only attacked her because of his great love for her.

The husband turns his head toward them. (28

275 *CU of the wife as she looks up as though she believes what Tajomaru is saying, her eyes dreamy.*

SAMURAI-MEDIUM (*off*): My wife looked at him, her face soft, her eyes veiled. (8

276 *CU of the medium in the prison courtyard, as at the end of shot 273.*

SAMURAI-MEDIUM: Never, in all of our life together, had I seen her more beautiful. (6

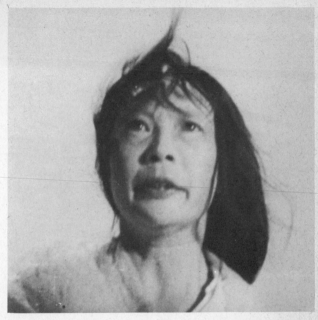

277 *CU of the husband in the woods; he stares at the others, then closes his eyes.*

SAMURAI-MEDIUM (*off*): And what did my beautiful wife reply to the bandit in front of her helpless husband? (17

278 *MS. The woman looks up at Tajomaru, imploringly.*

WOMAN: Take me. Take me away with you. (11

279 *CU of the medium in the prison courtyard; she rises, the wind whipping her hair. The unearthly voice fades in and out.*

SAMURAI-MEDIUM: That is what she said. (*The medium turns away, then abruptly faces the camera again.*) But that is not all she did, or else I would not now be in darkness. (15

280 MS, in the woods, from behind the husband's back. Tajomaru picks up the husband's sword and moves off screen. He returns, leading the woman off into the woods. (10

281 CU of Tajomaru as he is jerked to a stop by the woman. (2

282 MS of the woman holding Tajomaru by the hand. She points toward her husband.

WOMAN: Kill him. As long as he is alive I cannot go with you. (*She moves behind Tajomaru, clutching him*.) Kill him! *(12*

283 *MS of the medium in the prison courtyard, the wind howling about her.*

SAMURAI-MEDIUM: I still hear those words. (*The medium writhes in circles on her knees*.) They are like a wind blowing me to the bottom of this dark pit. Has anyone ever uttered more pitiless words? Even the bandit was shocked to hear them. *(25*

284 *ECU of the woman in the woods, clinging to the bandit's shoulder, digging her nails into him.*

WOMAN: Kill him! (7

285 *LS from behind the husband's back; the woman*

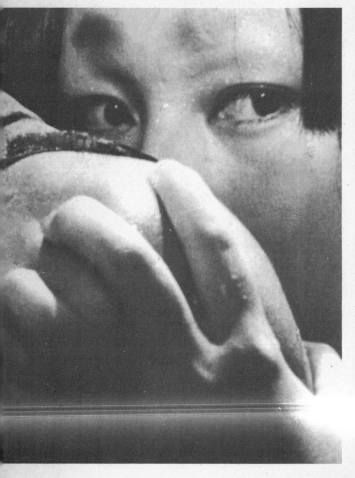

takes a step toward the husband, pointing at him.
WOMAN: Kill him—kill him!   (10

286 *CU of Tajomaru, yanking the woman back to him.*
The look in his eyes makes her back off.   (8

287 (=285) *LS. The bandit throws the woman from him.* (2

288 *MS of the woman as she falls to the ground; the bandit places his foot on her back.* (3

289 *CU of the medium in the prison courtyard. She throws her head back and then forward and the dead man's laughter pours from her unmoving lips.* (5

290 (=285) *LS. Tajomaru, still standing over the woman, addresses the husband.*

TAJOMARU: What do you want me to do with this woman? Kill her? Spare her? Just nod if you agree.

The camera dollies around to show the husband in profile.

SAMURAI-MEDIUM (*off*): For these words I almost forgave the bandit. (27

291 *LS of the husband in the background; in the fore-*

ground (MS) Tajomaru continues pressing the woman to the ground with his foot.

TAJOMARU: What do you want me to do? Kill her? Let her go?

Now Tajomaru walks toward the husband. As soon as he has gone a few steps, the woman springs up and runs away. Tajomaru turns to chase her, the camera panning to show them disappear among the trees. Her screams die away in the stillness of the woods. (18

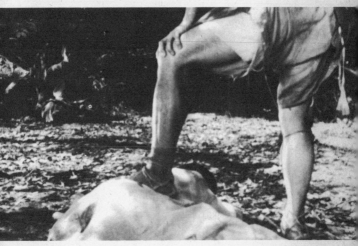

292 *LS of the husband; still bound, he makes no effort to free himself.* (9

293 *MS of the husband.* (6

294 *CU of the husband.* (4

295 *Dead leaves on the ground in the late afternoon sun.*

SAMURAI-MEDIUM (*off*): Hours later—I don't know how many. (5

296 *MS of the husband's back. Tajomaru appears in the background, on the far side of the clearing, stomping along, slashing in disgust with some rope at the bushes. He walks up to the husband and stands looking down.* (27

297 *MS from reverse angle. Tajomaru takes his sword and cuts the captive's bonds.*

TAJOMARU: Well, she got away. Now I'll have to worry about her talking. (*He turns and goes.*)

The husband looks off after him, then up at the sky. (45

298 *Trees against the sky.*

SAMURAI-MEDIUM (*off*): It was quiet. (4

299 *Dead leaves on the ground.*

SAMURAI-MEDIUM (*off*): Then I heard someone crying . . .

The camera tilts up along the leaves to reveal the husband (MS). The bell-like tinkle of wind chimes is heard. (11

300 *CU of the husband crying. The camera dollies back and he rises to his feet. He moves painfully (pan), rests his head against a tree. There is the soft sound of grief, but it comes from the husband himself.* (39

301 *CU as he rests his head against the tree, sobbing. Finally he raises his head and begins to wander off, but stops when he notices something on the ground.* (28

302 *MS from behind the husband, the dagger sticking up before him. Slowly he goes to it, picks it up, and turns to walk back toward the camera, staring at the dagger.* (32

303 *LS as he moves into the clearing; he stops, raises the dagger high above his head and brutally thrusts it into his chest. He begins to fall.* (16

304 *MS. His falling motion is completed by the medium in the prison courtyard (priest and woodcutter sit in the background). The medium sinks down as though dead, then slowly sits up.* (21

305 *CU of the medium.*

SAMURAI-MEDIUM: Everything was quiet—how quiet it was. It grew dark and a mist seemed to envelop me. I lay quietly in this stillness. Then someone

seemed to approach me. Softly, gently. Who could it have been? Then someone's hand grasped the dagger and drew it out. (*The medium falls forward.*)

Music up and out. (59

306 *LS. In the shelter of the Rashomon, the priest and commoner are seated at the fire; the woodcutter is pacing up and down, the camera panning with him. (18*

307 *MS as the woodcutter stops in the background and turns to the others.*

WOODCUTTER: That's not true. There wasn't any dagger there—he was killed by a sword.

The commoner looks up from tending the fire. The woodcutter, very agitated, moves farther into the background and sits down; the commoner rises and goes back to sit beside him. (40

308 *MS from reverse angle. The commoner sits next to the woodcutter; the priest is in the background.*

COMMONER: Now it's getting interesting. You must have seen the whole thing. Why didn't you tell the police?

WOODCUTTER: I didn't want to get involved.

COMMONER: But now you want to talk about it? Well, come on and tell us then. Yours seems the most interesting of all these stories. (32

309 *MS from reverse angle, the priest in the foreground.*

PRIEST: I don't want to hear. I don't want to have to listen to any more horrible stories.

The commoner stands and comes forward to the priest.

COMMONER (*to the priest*): Stories like this are ordinary enough now. I heard that demons used to live in the castle here by the gate, but they all ran away, because what men do now horrified them so. (*He goes back to the woodcutter.*) (17

310 *CU of the woodcutter and commoner.*

COMMONER: How much do you know about this story?
WOODCUTTER: I found a woman's hat . . .
COMMONER: You already said that.
WOODCUTTER: Then, when I'd walked about twenty

yards farther, I heard a woman crying. I looked out from behind a bush and saw a man tied up. There was a woman crying. And there was Tajomaru.

COMMONER: Wait a minute. Then it was a lie when you said that you found the body?

WOODCUTTER: I didn't want to get involved.

COMMONER: All right, then. Go on. What was Tajomaru doing?

WOODCUTTER: He was down on his knees in front of the woman and seemed to be begging her to forgive him. *(57*

311 *MS. The woods. Tajomaru crouches by the woman, the samurai behind them. She is sobbing. From the beginning to the end of the woodcutter's story, there is a noticeable absence of music. The only sounds heard, aside from those made by the three people, are occasional noises natural to the woods.*

TAJOMARU: Until now, whenever I wanted to do anything bad, I always did it. It was for me and so it was good. But today is different. I've already taken you, but now I want you more and more—and I suffer. Go away with me. If you want, I'll marry you. Look. (*He bows his head low.*) I am Tajomaru, the famous bandit, known all over Miyako, and yet here I am on my knees in front of you. *(38*

312 *MS from the side. Tajomaru puts his hand on her, trying to soothe her.*

TAJOMARU: If you want, I'll even stop being a bandit. I've got enough money hidden away. You can live comfortably. And if you don't want me to steal, then I'll work hard—I'll even sell things in the street. I'll make you happy. I'll do anything to please you if you'll only come away with me, marry me. (*She only sobs the harder.*) *(27*

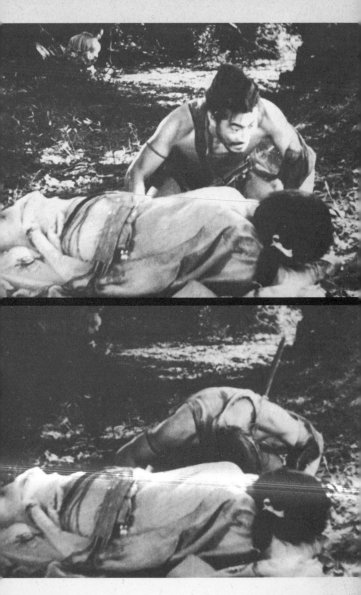

313 *CU from same angle as shot 311. Now the bandit tries to cajole her.*

TAJOMARU: Please say yes. If you don't, I'll have to kill you. *(13*

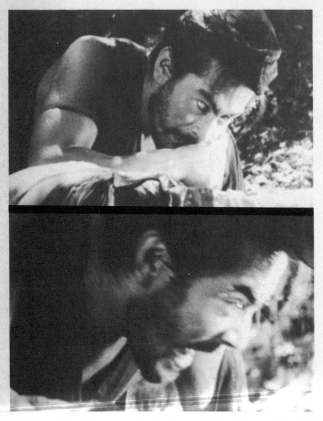

314 *ECU of Tajomaru; he is becoming desperate.*

TAJOMARU: Don't cry. Answer. Tell me you'll be my wife. (*Unable to endure her silence, he suddenly pushes her.*) *(9*

315 *ECU from over Tajomaru's shoulder. He bends over solicitously again.*
TAJOMARU: Tell me. (8

316 *CU from reverse angle. She sits up, almost in possession of herself.*

WOMAN: But, how could I answer? How could I, a woman, answer a question like that? (*She rises on her knees, the camera panning as she crawls over to the dagger and yanks it out of the ground.*) (19

317 *MS of the samurai, trussed up, in the foreground.
Tajomaru leaps aside and trips to the ground as the
woman spins around with the dagger in her hand. But
she is going to her husband with it. She cuts his bonds,
then backs away sobbing, stumbling, and falls to the
ground between the two men.* (12

318 *MS of Tajomaru, crouching on the ready.*

TAJOMARU: I understand. You mean that we men must
decide. (*He reaches for his sword.*) (7

319 *LS from behind Tajomaru. The samurai is strug-*

gling to free himself of the bonds now that the rope
has been cut. (2

320 *MS of the samurai as he jumps to his feet and
nervously backs away.*

SAMURAI (*holding up his hand in front of him*): Stop! I
refuse to risk my life for such a woman. (8

321 *CU. Tajomaru looks at him hesitantly.* (12

322 *CU. The woman sits up and looks in disbelief at
her husband.* (9

323 *MS. The samurai, now haughty and self-possessed, walks up to his wife.*

SAMURAI: You shameless whore! Why don't you kill yourself? *(19*

324 *MS from farther away, so that Tajomaru is visible
in the foreground.*

SAMURAI (*to Tajomaru*): If you want her, I'll give her
    to you. I regret the loss of my horse much more than

I will regret the loss of this woman. (*He turns away.*)
(11

325 *CU of the woman; shocked, she turns from her husband to look at the bandit.* (3

326 *MS. She stares up at Tajomaru, who looks from her to the samurai.* (7

327 *MS, the samurai in the foreground, Tajomaru*

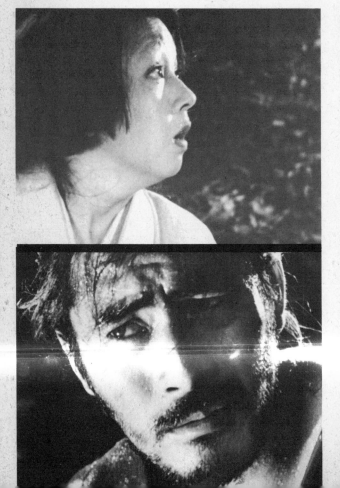

staring at him. The samurai looks from one to the other.
(17

328 *ECU. Tajomaru looks at the woman distrustfully.*
(4

329 *CU. She, sweating visibly, looks at Tajomaru.* *(8*

330 (=328) *CU. Tajomaru looks at her with distaste,*
wipes the sweat from his face. *(8*

331 *MS. She watches him cross behind her as if to go, then gets up and runs after him (pan), both of them passing the husband, who stands immobile.*

WOMAN: Wait!

Tajomaru turns and calls back.

TAJOMARU: And don't try to follow me. (13

332 *MS. Through Tajomaru's legs the woman is seen falling to the ground, her husband standing behind her. Then the husband steps forward.* (11

333 *MS of the husband.*

SAMURAI: Don't waste your time in crying. No matter how hard you cry no one is going to be taken in by it.

(5

334 *MS of Tajomaru as he steps forward to contradict.*

TAJOMARU: Don't talk like that to her. It's unmanly of you. After all, women cannot help crying. They are naturally weak.

(11

335 *CU of the woman on the ground. Her weeping has*

been heard behind Tajomaru's words; now the sobs change and she laughs. She rises, screeching with hysterical laughter.

WOMAN: It's not me, not me—it's you two who are

weak. (*Pan as she goes to her husband.*) If you are my husband then why don't you kill this man? Then you can tell me to kill myself. That is what a real man would do. But you aren't a real man. That is why I was crying. I'm tired, tired of this farce. (*Pan as she crosses to the bandit.*) I thought that Tajomaru might find some way out. I thought that if he would only save me I would do anything for him. (*70*

336 *CU of the woman and Tajomaru. She spits in his face, then backs off, laughing (pan).*

WOMAN: But he's not a man either. He's just like my husband! (*11*

337 *MS of Tajomaru, looking shamefaced.*
WOMAN (*off*): Just remember . . .   (5

338 (=335) *CU of the woman.*
WOMAN: . . . that a woman loves only a real man. (*She
moves nearer the bandit—pan.*) And when she loves,

she loves madly, forgetting everything else. But a woman can be won only by strength—by the strength (*she is now at Tajomaru's side*) of the swords you are wearing. *(11*

339 *MS of the husband. He looks at her abjectly, then reaches for his sword.* *(5*

340 *CU of the husband as he moves toward Tajomaru, now ready for a fight.* (1

341 *MS of all three; the woman and bandit, his sword already drawn, are in the foreground. From too far away, the samurai hurriedly swings his sword at Tajomaru, then backs quickly off. The woman smiles scornfully.* (3

342 *MS. The woman looks from one to the other, laughing and pointing gleefully.* (13

343 *LS. The two men, from high above, through the branches of the trees. They stand facing each other from a safe distance, the woman between them.* (7

344 *CU of the woman. She seems to realize what is happening and a frightened look comes over her face. The sound of the combatants' nervous panting is heard now, and runs throughout the fight scene. It is a tense, gasping sound, unrelieved by music or any sound other than the occasional clash of swords.* (10

345 *MS of the bandit, circling, feinting, a concerned expression on his face.* (9

346 *MS of the samurai, advancing uncertainly.* (13

347 (=345) *MS of the bandit advancing.* (3

348 (=346) *MS of the samurai advancing.* (2

349 *CU of the woman, watching fearfully. The camera dollies back until the two raised swords are visible in the frame. Suddenly the tips of the swords touch.* (16

350 *LS. The men recoil from the touching of the swords, stumbling backward away from each other. The samurai trips to the ground. Tajomaru runs after the samurai, but falls down himself. Both men swing wildly and blindly as they get to their feet and run in opposite directions from each other.* (7

351 *LS. Tajomaru in the foreground. The men are separated now by a great distance.* (5

352 CU of the woman as she peeks out from behind the stump of a tree. (14

353 MS of the samurai, who has fallen against the side of a slope. Finally he stands up and advances. (17

354 MS. Back-tracking shot of Tajomaru, advancing fearfully. His arm shaking violently, he seems almost unable to bear the weight of the sword. His breath comes in short gasps. (14

355 (=353) MS of the samurai advancing, terror written on his face. (2

356 (=354) MS of Tajomaru advancing. (2

357 *CU of the woman, terrified; the camera dollies back as the men enter from either side of the frame. Each thrusts, frightening the other, but this time the samurai turns to run first, and Tajomaru pursues him over to the slope (pan).* **(17**

358 *MS. They both slip and fall on the slope. Tajomaru thrusts at the samurai but misses, and his sword sticks in the ground. He can't extract it. Now the samurai swings, but the bandit rolls out of the way.* **(5**

359 *LS. Tajomaru continues to roll away (pan) to another part of the slope, which he tries to crawl up but fails to get a handhold.* **(6**

360 *CU as Tajomaru dodges another thrust.* **(1**

361 *MS. The samurai scampers after him but keeps stumbling and missing with his flailing swings.* (10

362 *MS. The bandit gets back to his sword but still can't pull it out. The samurai keeps lunging and missing; Tajomaru keeps dodging.* (27

363 *LS. The bandit runs and makes another attempt to mount the rise but falls (pan). Now he runs away from the slope (pan) and falls by a tree stump. The samurai aims another stroke wildly as Tajomaru falls behind the stump.* (16

364 *MS. The samurai's sword lodges itself in the stump; Tajomaru seizes the opportunity by leaping up at his assailant and pushing him down.* (1

365 *MS. Tajomaru tries to run past the fallen man but the samurai grabs him by the ankle and pulls him down. Dragging the samurai after him, Tajomaru begins to inch toward his own sword.* (9

366 *MS from reverse angle. Slowly and with great effort, the bandit inches toward his sword, the samurai holding onto his foot. Then Tajomaru kicks him away and at last frees the sword from the ground.* (20

367 *MS. The samurai, still on the ground, backs off in alarm.* (6

368 *MS. Tajomaru, out of breath, rises shakily.* (9

369 *LS. Pan as Tajomaru advances on the samurai, who pushes himself along on his hands farther and farther into a thicket. Dolly in on the trapped man, who screams.*

SAMURAI: I don't want to die! I don't want to die!

Pan to Tajomaru raising his sword and hurling it, out of frame, into the man lying in front of him. Then he whirls around triumphantly. (73

370 *LS. Tajomaru in the foreground, the woman cowering in the background. He backs away from the body*

and stumbles to the ground in front of the woman. (20

371 *MS of Tajomaru and the woman. They stare over at the body. Tajomaru, an idiotic expression on his face, rises and takes her hands, but she pulls them away and begins to back off frantically (pan), ending near the tree stump in which her husband's sword is still lodged. She utters little inarticulate cries. Tajomaru has followed stupidly, and now, half-crazed, he pulls the dead man's sword free and swings it mightily at her as she flees.* (38

372 *LS. She rushes off into the woods; he follows but trips. She disappears as he lies collapsed on the ground.* (22

373 *MS of Tajomaru's back. He sits up slowly, breathing hard, dirty, sweaty, exhausted. Silence—then the sound of distant cicada.* (9

374 LS as he sits stupefied. After a long time, he gets to his feet and goes off, to where the body lies, reappearing a moment later with his own bloody sword as well as the samurai's. (43

375 MS. Dragging the swords along, Tajomaru backs off and limps away into the woods. (21

376 *LS. The Rashomon. The three men sitting, framed overhead by a huge horizontal beam. The sound of the great downpour. The commoner laughs.* (5

377 *MS. The priest is in the foreground. The commoner stands.*

COMMONER: And I suppose that is supposed to be true.

WOODCUTTER (*getting to his feet*): I don't tell lies. I saw it with my own eyes.

COMMONER: That I doubt.

WOODCUTTER: I don't tell lies.

COMMONER: Well, so far as that goes, no one tells lies after he has said that he's going to tell one.

PRIEST: But it's horrible. If men don't trust one another then the earth becomes a kind of hell.

COMMONER: You are right. The world we live in is a hell.

PRIEST: No. I trust men. (*He turns away from the commoner and rises.*)   (23

378 *CU of the priest, standing by a column.*

PRIEST: But I don't want to believe that this world is a hell.

The commoner appears behind him, laughing.

COMMONER: No one will hear you, no matter how loud you shout. Just think now. Which one of these stories do you believe?

Before the priest can answer, the woodcutter begins to speak. As he does the camera pans past the column to a MS of him.

WOODCUTTER: I don't understand any of them. They don't make any sense.

The commoner steps forward from behind the column and goes up to the woodcutter.

COMMONER: Well, don't worry about it. It isn't as though men were reasonable. (*He turns to walk off.*)
(23

379 *LS. The commoner walks to the fire he has built, squats, and throws several of the burning pieces of lumber out into the rain. Just then the cry of a baby is heard. All look around. The commoner stands up.* (23

380 MS. The three men try to locate the source of the crying. Then the commoner runs to the back and heads behind a partition of the gate. The priest and the woodcutter look at each other, then run over to the broken panels of the partition (pan) and peer through to where the woodcutter has disappeared. (19

381 MS from the other side of the partition. The heads of the two men appear through openings in the panels; in the distance, the commoner is kneeling over the baby, stripping off its few clothes. (4

382 MS of the commoner as he finishes removing the clothes and examines them. (8

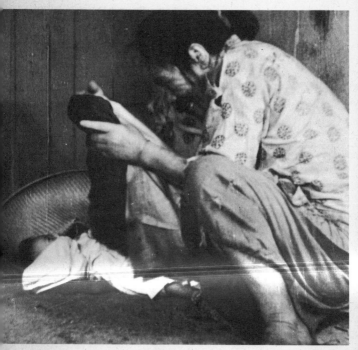

383 *MS of the priest and woodcutter watching; they dash around the partition (pan), the priest picking up the infant and the woodcutter going up to the commoner and pushing him.*

WOODCUTTER: What are you doing?
COMMONER: What does it look like? (14

384 *CU of the priest holding the baby protectively.* (1

385 *MS of the three men, priest in the background, commoner partially hidden by some steps (shot from a low angle).*

WOODCUTTER: That's horrible.
COMMONER: What's so horrible about it? Somebody

else would have taken those baby clothes if I hadn't. Why shouldn't it be me?

WOODCUTTER: You are evil.

COMMONER: Evil? Me? And if so, then what are the parents of that baby? (*Pan as he moves up close to the woodcutter.*) They had a good time making it— then they throw it away like this. That's real evil for you.

WOODCUTTER: No, you're wrong. Look! Look here at the amulet case it has on. It's something the parents left to guard over it. Think what they must have gone through to give this baby up.

COMMONER: Oh, well. If you're going to sympathize with other people . . .

WOODCUTTER: Selfish . . .

COMMONER: And what's wrong with that? That's the way we are, the way we live. Look, half of us envy the lives that dogs lead. You just can't live unless you're what you call "selfish."

The commoner turns and goes off. The woodcutter moves into CU.

WOODCUTTER: Brute! (*With gathering anger.*) All men are selfish and dishonest. They all have excuses. The bandit, the husband . . . you! (*His face distorted in anger, he leaps in the direction of the commoner.*)   (77

386 *CU as the woodcutter grabs the commoner by the neck and shakes him; they struggle out into the rain, and continue to argue there.*

COMMONER: And you say you don't lie! That's just funny. Look, you may have fooled the police, but you don't fool me.   (15

387 *CU from reverse angle, the woodcutter facing the camera now. The commoner's words have affected the woodcutter. Guiltily he lets go his hold on the commoner.*   (7

388 *CU from reverse angle. The commoner smiles, then shoves the woodcutter; he comes forward and shoves him again, this time out of frame. Smiling, the commoner follows him out.*   (9

389 *MS of the two men back under the roof, out of the rain. As the commoner speaks, he continues to shove the woodcutter back (pan), finally pushing him against the partition near the priest.*

COMMONER: And so where is that dagger? That pearl-inlay handle that the bandit said was so valuable? Did the earth open up and swallow it? Or did someone steal it? Am I right? It would seem so. Now *there* is a really selfish action for you. (*He slaps the woodcutter and laughs harshly.*) (34

390 *CU of the priest holding the baby.* (3

391 *LS of all three men.*

COMMONER: Anything else you want to tell me? If not, I think I'll be going.

The baby starts to cry. The commoner glances at it; then, laughing, he turns to go. (19

392 *LS from outside the gate. The commoner comes out in the rain toward the camera and disappears off. The other two remain under the gate, seen in LS through the rain. (Dissolve.)* (19

393 *MS. The two men, from closer; the sound of the rain diminishes. (Dissolve.)* (11

394 *MS. The two men, closer yet; rain slowly stopping. (Dissolve.)* (9

395 *CU. The two men still standing as before; the sound of rain has stopped; the baby cries.* (7

396 *LS. The two men seen from outside the gate as in shot 392, but now the rain has stopped. Drops of water drip from the gate onto the steps. The priest steps forward.* (11

397 *MS. He walks past the woodcutter, patting the baby, and leaves the frame. The woodcutter stands for a moment, then follows.* (11

398 *MS. The woodcutter approaches the priest and moves to take the baby away from him; the priest violently resists.*

PRIEST: What are you trying to do? Take away what little it has left? (7

399 *MS. Priest in the foreground. The woodcutter, very humble now, shakes his head.*

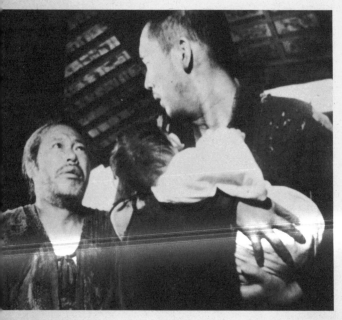

WOODCUTTER: I have six children of my own. One more wouldn't make it any more difficult. (29

400 *MS from reverse angle; woodcutter in the foreground.*

PRIEST: I'm sorry. I shouldn't have said that. (10

401 (=399) *MS. Priest in the foreground.*

WOODCUTTER: Oh, you can't afford not to be suspicious of people these days. I'm the one who ought to be ashamed. (23

402 (=400) *MS. Woodcutter in the foreground.*

PRIEST: No, I'm grateful to you. Because, thanks to you, I think I will be able to keep my faith in men. (27

403 (=399) *MS. Priest in the foreground. The wood-cutter bows, and the baby, who has been crying all during this dialogue, stops. The priest holds out the baby and the woodcutter takes it. Finale music begins, a distinctly traditional Japanese music.* (7

404 *MS from farther back. The woodcutter accepts the baby and steps back. The men bow to each other and the woodcutter turns to go.* (27

405 *LS from behind the men as the woodcutter, holding the infant, leaves the gate; the sky is clear, the priest watches as he goes.* (11

406 *LS from reverse angle. The woodcutter moves to-*
ward the camera. He stops and bows again to the
priest. Then he turns and continues on his way, the
camera tracking backward with him. The whole gate
and the sunny sky come into frame. The woodcutter

walks past the camera; the tracking stops and the
priest is seen, small, standing under the gate.   (49

407 The great signboard of the gate. Music up and
out.   (9

Akira Kurosawa

Credits

The credits for the film are superimposed over the opening shots of the gate.

A Daiei Production
Written by Shinobu Hashimoto and Akira Kurosawa
After two stories by Ryunosuke Akutagawa
Photographed by Kazuo Miyagawa
Art direction by So Matsuyama
Music by Fumio Hayasaka
Lighting by Kenichi Okamoto
Produced by Jingo Minoru
Directed by Akira Kurosawa

Tajomaru, the bandit	Toshiro Mifune
Takehiro, the samurai	Masayuki Mori
Masago, his wife	Machiko Kyo
The woodcutter	Takashi Shimura
The priest	Minoru Chiaki
The commoner	Kichijiro Ueda
The police agent	Daisuke Kato
The medium	Fumiko Homma

Running time: 88 minutes.

Premiere: August 25, 1950, Tokyo; December 26, 1951, New York.

U.S. distributor: initially, RKO; subsequently, Edward Harrison; now, Janus Films.

Prizes: Grand Prize, Venice Festival, 1951.
Academy Award, Best Foreign Film, 1952.

The Akutagawa Stories

Rashomon

It was a chilly evening. A samurai's servant stood under the Rashomon,* waiting for a break in the rain.

No one else was under the wide gate. On the thick column, its crimson lacquer rubbed off here and there, perched a cricket. Since the Rashomon stands on Sujaku Avenue, a few other people at least, in sedge hat or nobleman's headgear, might have been expected to be waiting there for a break in the rainstorm. But no one was near except this man.

For the past few years the city of Kyoto had been visited by a series of calamities, earthquakes, whirl-winds, and fires, and Kyoto had been greatly devastated. Old chronicles say that broken pieces of Buddhist images and other Buddhist objects, with their lacquer, gold, or silver leaf worn off, were heaped up on roadsides to be sold as firewood. Such being the state of affairs in Kyoto, the repair of the Rashomon was out of the question. Taking advantage of the devastation, foxes and other wild animals made their dens in the ruins of the gate, and thieves and robbers found a home there too. Eventually it became customary to bring unclaimed corpses to this gate and abandon them. After dark it was so ghostly that no one dared approach.

Flocks of crows flew in from somewhere. During the daytime these cawing birds circled round the ridgepole of the gate. When the sky overhead turned red in the afterlight of the departed sun, they looked like so

---

The "Rashomon" was the largest gate in Kyoto, the ancient capital of Japan. It was 106 feet wide and 26 feet deep, and was topped with a ridgepole; its stone wall rose 75 feet high. This gate was constructed in 789, and in 794 the capital of Japan was transferred to Kyoto. With the decline of Kyoto in the twelfth century, the gate fell into disrepair, crack-ing and crumbling in many places.

many grains of sesame flung across the gate. But on that day not a crow was to be seen, perhaps because of the lateness of the hour. Here and there the stone steps, beginning to crumble, and with rank grass growing in their crevices, were dotted with the white droppings of crows. The servant, in a worn blue kimono, sat on the seventh and highest step, vacantly watching the rain. His attention was drawn to a large pimple irritating his right cheek.

As has been said, the servant was waiting for a break in the rain. But he had no particular idea of what to do after the rain stopped. Ordinarily, of course, he would have returned to his master's house, but he had been discharged just before. The prosperity of the city of Kyoto had been rapidly declining, and he had been dismissed by his master, whom he had served many years, because of the effects of this decline. Thus, confined by the rain, he was at a loss to know where to go. And the weather had not a little to do with his depressed mood. The rain seemed unlikely to stop. He was lost in thoughts of how to make his living tomorrow, helpless incoherent thoughts protesting an inexorable fate. Aimlessly he had been listening to the pattering of the rain on the Sujaku Avenue.

The rain, enveloping the Rashomon, gathered strength and came down with a pelting sound that could be heard far away. Looking up, he saw a fat black cloud impale itself on the tips of the tiles jutting out from the roof of the gate.

He had little choice of means, whether fair or foul, because of helpless circumstances. If he chose honest means, he would undoubtedly starve to death beside the wall or in the Sujaku gutter. He would be brought to this gate and thrown away like a stray dog. If he decided to steal . . . His mind, after making the same detour time and again, came finally to the conclusion that he would be a thief.

But doubts returned many times. Though determined

that he had no choice, he was still unable to muster enough courage to justify the conclusion that he must become a thief.

After a loud fit of sneezing he got up slowly. The evening chill of Kyoto made him long for the warmth of a brazier. The wind in the evening dusk howled through the columns of the gate. The cricket which had been perched on the crimson lacquered column was already gone.

Ducking his neck, he looked around the gate as he drew up the shoulders of the blue kimono which he wore over his thin undergarments. He decided to spend the night there, if he could find a secluded corner sheltered from wind and rain. He found a broad lacquered stairway leading to the tower over the gate. No one would be there, except the dead, if there were any. So, taking care that the sword at his side did not slip out of the scabbard, he set foot on the lowest step of the stairs.

A few seconds later, halfway up the stairs, he saw a movement above. Holding his breath and huddling cat-like in the middle of the broad stairs leading to the tower, he watched and waited. A light coming from the upper part of the tower shone faintly upon his right cheek. It was the cheek with the red, festering pimple visible under his stubby whiskers. He had expected only dead people inside the tower, but he had gone up only a few steps before he noticed a fire above, near which someone was moving. He saw a dull, yellow, flickering light which made the cobwebs hanging from the ceiling glow in a ghostly way. What sort of person would be making a fire in the Rashomon . . . and in a storm? The unknown, the evil terrified him.

Quietly as a lizard, the servant crept up to the top of the steep stairs. Crouching on all fours and stretching his neck as far as possible, he timidly peered into the tower.

As rumor had said, he found several corpses strewn

carelessly about the floor. Since the glow of the light was feeble, he could not count the number. He could only see that some were naked and others clothed. Some were women, and all were sprawled on the floor with their mouths open or their arms outstretched, showing no more sign of life than so many clay dolls. One would doubt that they had ever been alive, so eternally silent were they. Their shoulders, breasts, and torsos stood out in the dim light; other parts vanished in shadow. The offensive smell of these decomposed corpses brought his hand to his nose.

The next moment his hand dropped and he stared. He caught sight of a ghoulish form bent over a corpse. It seemed to be an old woman, gaunt, gray-haired, and nunnish in appearance. With a pine torch in her right hand, she was gazing into the face of a corpse which had long black hair.

Seized more with horror than curiosity, he drew no breath for a time. He felt the hair of his head and body stand on end. As he watched, terrified, she wedged the torch between two floor boards and, laying hands on the head of the corpse, began to pull out the long hairs one by one, as a monkey kills the lice of her young. The hair came out smoothly with the movement of her hands.

As the hair came out, fear faded from his heart, and his hatred toward the old woman mounted. It grew beyond hatred, becoming a consuming antipathy against all evil. At this instant if anyone had brought up the question of whether he would starve to death or become a thief—the question which had occurred to him a little while ago—he would not have hesitated to choose death. His hatred of evil flared up like the piece of pine wood which the old woman had stuck in the floor.

He did not know why she pulled out the hair of the dead. Accordingly, he did not know whether her case was to be judged as good or bad. But in his eyes, pulling out the hair of the dead in the Rashomon on this stormy night was an unpardonable crime. Of course it never entered his mind that a little while ago he had thought of becoming a thief.

Then, summoning strength into his legs, he rose from the stairs and strode, hand on sword, right in front of the old creature. The hag turned, terror in her eyes, and sprang up from the floor, trembling. For a moment she paused, poised there, then lunged for the stairs with a shriek.

"Wretch! Where are you going?" he shouted, barring the way of the trembling hag who tried to scurry past him. Still she attempted to claw her way by. He pushed her back to prevent her. . . . They struggled, fell among the corpses, and grappled there. The issue was never in doubt. In a moment he had her by the arm, twisted it, and forced her down to the floor. Her arms were nothing but skin and bones, and there was no more flesh on them than on the shanks of a chicken. No sooner was she on the floor than he drew his sword and thrust the silver-white blade before her very nose. She was silent. She trembled as if in a fit, and her eyes were open so wide that they were almost out of their sockets, and her breath came in hoarse gasps. The life of this wretch was his now. This thought cooled his boiling anger and brought a calm pride and satisfaction. He looked down at her, and said in a somewhat calmer voice:

"Look here, I'm not an officer of the High Police Commissioner. I'm a stranger who happened to pass by this gate. I won't bind you or do anything against you, but you must tell me what you're doing up here."

Then the old woman opened her eyes still wider, and gazed at his face intently with the sharp red eyes of a bird of prey. She moved her lips, which were wrinkled into her nose, as though she were chewing something. Her pointed Adam's apple moved in her thin throat. Then a panting sound like the cawing of a crow came from her throat:

"I pull the hair . . . I pull out the hair . . . to make a wig."

Her answer banished the unknown from their encounter and brought disappointment. Suddenly she was merely a trembling old woman there at his feet. A ghoul no longer: only a hag who makes wigs from the hair of the dead—to sell, for scraps of food. A cold contempt seized him. Fear left his heart, and his former hatred returned. These feelings must have been sensed by the other. The old creature, still clutching the hair she had pulled from the corpse, mumbled out these words in her harsh broken voice:

"Indeed, making wigs out of the hair of the dead may seem a great evil to you, but these that are here deserve no better. This woman, whose beautiful black hair I was pulling, used to sell dried snake flesh at the guard barracks, saying that it was dried fish. If she hadn't died of the plague, she'd be selling it now. The guards liked to buy from her, and used to say her fish was tasty. What she did couldn't be wrong, because if she hadn't, she would have starved to death. There was no other choice. If she knew I had to do this in order to live, she probably wouldn't care."

He sheathed his sword, and, with his left hand on its hilt, he listened to her meditatively. His right hand touched the big pimple on his cheek. As he listened, a certain courage was born in his heart—the courage he had not had when he sat under the gate a little while ago. A strange power was driving him in the opposite direction from the courage he had had when he seized the old woman. No longer did he wonder whether he should starve to death or become a thief. Starvation was so far from his mind that it was the last thing that would have entered it.

"Are you sure?" he asked in a mocking tone, when

she finished talking. He took his right hand from his pimple, and, bending forward, seized her by the neck and said sharply:

"Then it's right if I rob you. I'd starve if I didn't."

He tore her clothes from her body and kicked her roughly down on the corpses as she struggled and tried to clutch his leg. Five steps, and he was at the top of the stairs. The yellow clothes he had wrested from her were under his arm, and in a twinkling he had rushed down the steep stairs into the abyss of night. The thunder of his descending steps pounded in the hollow tower, and then it was quiet.

In a Grove

*The Testimony of a Woodcutter Questioned
by a High Police Commissioner*

Yes, sir. Certainly, it was I who found the body. This
morning, as usual, I went to cut my daily quota of
cedars, when I found the body in a grove in a hollow in
the mountains.

The exact location? About 150 yards off the Yamashina stage road. It's an out-of-the-way grove of bamboo and cedars.

The body was lying flat on its back dressed in a
bluish silk kimono and a wrinkléd headdress of the
Kyoto style. A single sword stroke had pierced the
breast. The fallen bamboo blades around it were
stained with bloody blossoms.

No, the blood was no longer flowing. The wound had
dried up, I believe. And also, a gadfly was stuck fast
there, hardly noticing my footsteps.

You ask me if I saw a sword or any such thing? No,
nothing, sir. I found only a rope at the root of a cedar
nearby. And . . . well, in addition to a rope, I found a
comb. That was all. Apparently he must have made a
battle of it before he was murdered, because the grass
and fallen bamboo blades had been trampled down
all around.

A horse was nearby? No, sir. It's hard enough for
a man to enter, let alone a horse.

*The Testimony of a Traveling Buddhist Priest
Questioned by a High Police Commissioner*

The time? Certainly, it was about noon yesterday, sir.
The unfortunate man was on the road from Sekiyama
to Yamashina. He was walking toward Sekiyama with
a woman accompanying him on horseback, who I have

since learned was his wife. A scarf hanging from her head hid her face from view. All I saw was the color of her clothes, a lilac-colored suit. Her horse was a sorrel with a fine mane.

The lady's height? Oh, about four feet five inches. Since I am a Buddhist priest, I took little notice about her details. Well, the man was armed with a sword as well as a bow and arrows. And I remember that he carried some twenty-odd arrows in his quiver.

Little did I expect that he would meet such a fate. Truly, human life is as evanescent as the morning dew or a flash of lightning. My words are inadequate to express my sympathy for him.

The Testimony of a Policeman Questioned by a High Police Commissioner

The man that I arrested? He is a notorious brigand called Tajomaru. When I arrested him, he had fallen off his horse. He was groaning on the bridge at Awataguchi.

The time? It was in the early hours of last night. For the record, I might say that the other day I tried to arrest him, but unfortunately he escaped. He was wearing a dark-blue silk kimono and a large plain sword. And, as you see, he got a bow and arrows somewhere.

You say that this bow and these arrows look like the ones owned by the dead man? Then Tajomaru must be the murderer. The bow wound with leather strips, the black lacquered quiver, the seventeen arrows with hawk feathers—these were all in his possession, I believe.

Yes, sir, the horse is, as you say, a sorrel with a fine mane. A little beyond the stone bridge I found the horse grazing by the roadside, with his long rein dangling. Surely there is some providence in his having been thrown by the horse.

Of all the robbers prowling around Kyoto, this Tajomaru has brought the most grief to the women in town. Last autumn a wife who came to the mountain behind the Pindora of the Toribe Temple, presumably to pay a visit, was murdered, along with a girl. It has been suspected that it was his doing. If this criminal murdered the man, you cannot tell what he may have done with the man's wife. May it please your honor to look into this problem as well.

The Testimony of an Old Woman Questioned by a High Police Commissioner

Yes, sir, that corpse is the man who married my daughter. He does not come from Kyoto. He was a samurai in the town of Kokufu in the province of Wakasa. His name was Kanazawa no Takehiro, and his age was twenty-six. He was of a gentle disposition, so I am sure he did nothing to provoke the anger of others.

My daughter? Her name is Masago, and her age is nineteen. She is a spirited, fun-loving girl, but I am sure she has never known any man except Takehiro. She has a small, oval, dark-complexioned face with a mole at the corner of her left eye.

Yesterday Takehiro left for Wakasa with my daughter. What a misfortune that things should have come to such a sad end! What has become of my daughter? I am resigned to giving up my son-in-law as lost, but the fate of my daughter worries me sick. For heaven's sake, leave no stone unturned to find her. I hate that robber Tajomaru, or whatever his name is. Not only my son-in-law, but my daughter . . . (Her later words were drowned in tears.)

Tajomaru's Confession

I killed him, but not her.

Where's she gone? I can't tell. Oh, wait a minute. No torture can make me confess what I don't know. Now things have come to such a head, I won't keep anything from you.

Yesterday a little past noon I met that couple. Just then a puff of wind blew, and raised her hanging scarf, so that I caught a glimpse of her face. Instantly it was again covered from my view. That may have been one reason; she looked like a Bodhisattva. At that moment I had made up my mind to capture her even if I had to kill her man.

Why? To me killing isn't a matter of such great consequence as you might think. When a woman is captured, her man has to be killed anyway. In killing, I use the sword I wear at my side. Am I the only one who kills people? You, you don't use your swords. You kill people with your power, with your money. Sometimes you kill them on the pretext of working for their good. It's true they don't bleed. They are in the best of health, but all the same you've killed them. It's hard to say who is a greater sinner, you or me. (An ironical smile.)

But it would be good if I could capture a woman without killing her man. So I made up my mind to capture her, and do my best not to kill him. But it's out of the question on the Yamashina stage road, so I managed to lure the couple into the mountains.

It was quite easy. I became their traveling companion, and I told them there was an old mound in the mountain over there, and that I had dug it open and found many mirrors and swords. I went on to tell them I'd buried the things in a grove behind the mountain, and that I'd like to sell them at a low price to anyone who would care to have them. Then . . . you see, isn't greed terrible? He was beginning to be moved by my talk before he knew it. In less than half an hour they were driving their horse toward the mountain with me.

When he reached the grove, I told them that the treasures were buried in it, and I asked them to come and see. The man had no objection—he was blinded by greed. The woman said she would wait on horseback. It was natural for her to say so, at the sight of a thick grove. To tell you the truth, my plan worked just as I wished. So I went into the grove with him, leaving her behind alone.

The grove is only bamboo for some distance. About fifty yards ahead there's a rather open clump of cedars. It was a convenient spot for my purpose. Pushing my way through the grove, I told him a plausible lie that the treasures were buried under the cedars. When I told him this, he laboriously pushed his way toward the slender cedars visible through the grove. After a while the bamboo thinned out, and we came to where a number of cedars grew in a row. As soon as we got there, I seized him from behind. Because he was a trained, sword-bearing warrior, he was quite strong, but he was taken by surprise, so there was no help for him. I soon tied him up to the root of a cedar.

Where did I get a rope? Thank heaven, being a robber, I had rope with me, since I might have to scale a wall at any moment. Of course it was easy to stop him from calling out by gagging his mouth with fallen bamboo leaves.

When I disposed of him, I went to his woman and asked her to come and see him, because he seemed to have been suddenly taken sick. It's needless to say that this plan also worked well. The woman, her sedge hat off, came into the depths of the grove, where I led her by the hand. The instant she caught sight of her husband, she drew a small sword. I've never seen a woman of such violent temper. If I'd been off guard, I'd have got a thrust in my side. I dodged, but she kept on slashing at me. She might have wounded me deeply or killed me. But I'm Tajomaru. I managed to strike down her small sword without drawing my own. The most spirited woman is defenseless without a weapon. At last I could satisfy my desire for her without taking her husband's life.

Yes . . . without taking his life. I didn't want to kill him. I was about to run away from the grove, leaving the woman behind in tears, when she frantically clung to my arm. In broken fragments of words, she asked that either her husband or I die. She said it was more trying than death to have her shame known to two men. She gasped out that she wanted to be the wife of whichever survived. Then a furious desire to kill him seized me.

Telling you in this way, no doubt I seem a crueler man than you. But that's because you didn't see her face. Especially her burning eyes at that moment. As I saw her eye to eye, I wanted to make her my wife even if I were to be struck by lightning. I wanted to make her my wife . . . this single desire filled my mind. This was not simply lust, as you might think. At that time if I'd had no other desire than lust, I surely wouldn't have minded knocking her down and running away. Then I wouldn't have stained my sword with his blood. But the moment I gazed at her face in the dark grove, I decided not to leave without killing him.

But I didn't like to resort to unfair means to kill him. I untied him and told him to cross swords with me. The rope that was found at the root of the cedar is the rope I dropped at the time. Furious with anger, he drew his thick sword. And quick as a wink, he sprang at me ferociously, without speaking a word. I needn't tell you how our fight turned out. The twenty-third stroke . . . please remember this. I'm impressed with this fact still. Nobody under the sun has ever clashed swords with me twenty strokes. (A cheerful smile.)

When he fell, I turned toward her, lowering my blood-stained sword. But to my great astonishment she was gone. I wondered where she had run to. I looked for her in the clump of cedars. I listened, but heard only a groaning sound from the throat of the dying man.

As soon as we crossed swords, she may have run away through the grove to call for help. When I thought of that, I decided it was a matter of life and death to me. So, robbing him of his sword, and bow and arrows, I ran out to the mountain road. There I found her horse still grazing quietly. It would be a waste of words to tell you the later details, but before I entered town I had already parted with the sword. That's my confession. I know that my head will be hung in chains anyway, so give me the maximum penalty. (A defiant attitude.)

The Confession of a Woman Who Has Come to the Shimizu Temple

That man in the blue silk kimono, after forcing me to yield to him, laughed mockingly as he looked at my bound husband. How horrified my husband must have been! But no matter how hard he struggled in agony, the rope cut into him all the more tightly. In spite of myself I ran stumblingly toward his side. Or rather I tried to run toward him, but the man knocked me down. Just at that moment I saw an indescribable light in my husband's eyes. Something beyond expression . . . his eyes make me shudder even now. That instantaneous look of my husband, who couldn't speak a word, told me all his heart. The flash in his eyes was neither anger nor sorrow . . . only a cold light, a look of loathing. More struck by the look in his eyes than by the blow of the thief, I called out in spite of myself and fell unconscious.

In the course of time I came to, and found that the man in blue silk was gone. I saw only my husband still bound to the root of the cedar. I raised myself from the bamboo blades with difficulty, and looked into his face; but the expression in his eyes was just the same as before.

Beneath the cold contempt in his eyes, there was hatred. Shame, grief, and anger . . . I don't know how to express my heart at that time. Reeling to my feet, I went up to my husband.

"Takehiro," I said to him, "since things have come to this pass, I cannot live with you. I'm determined to die

. . . but you must die, too. You saw my shame. I can't leave you alive as you are."

This was all I could say. Still he went on gazing at me with loathing and contempt. My heart breaking, I looked for his sword. It must have been taken by the robber. Neither his sword nor his bow and arrow were to be seen in the grove. But fortunately my small sword was lying at my feet. Raising it overhead, once more I said, "Now give me your life. I'll follow you right away."

When he heard these words, he moved his lips with difficulty. Since his mouth was stuffed with leaves, of course his voice could not be heard. But at a glance I understood his words. Despising me, his look said only, "Kill me." Neither conscious nor unconscious, I stabbed the small sword through the lilac-colored kimono into his breast.

Again at this time I must have fainted. By the time I managed to look up, he had already breathed his last—still in bonds. A streak of sinking sunlight streamed through the clump of cedars and bamboos, and shone on his pale face. Gulping down my sobs, I untied the rope from his dead body. And . . . and what has become of me since, I have no more strength to tell you. Anyway, I hadn't the strength to die. I stabbed my own throat with the small sword, I threw myself into a pond at the foot of the mountain, and I tried to kill myself in many ways. Unable to end my life, I am still living in dishonor. (A lonely smile.) Worthless as I am, I must have been forsaken even by the most merciful Kwannon. I killed my own husband. I was violated by the robber. Whatever can I do? Whatever can I . . . I . . . (Gradually, violent sobbing.)

*The Story of the Murdered Man, as Told
Through a Medium*

After violating my wife, the robber, sitting there, began to speak comforting words to her. Of course I couldn't speak. My whole body was tied fast to the root of a cedar. But meanwhile I winked at her many times, as much as to say, "Don't believe the robber." I wanted to convey some such meaning to her. But my wife, sitting dejectedly on the bamboo leaves, was staring at her lap. To all appearances, she was listening to his words. I was racked with jealousy. In the meantime the robber went on with his clever talk, from one subject to another. The robber finally made his brazen proposal. "Once your virtue is stained, you won't get along well with your husband, so won't you be my wife instead? It's my love for you that made me violent toward you."

While the criminal talked, my wife raised her face as if in a trance. She had never looked so beautiful as at that moment. What did my beautiful wife say in answer to him while I was sitting bound there? I am lost in space, but I have never thought of her answer without burning with anger and jealousy. Truly she said, "Then take me away with you wherever you go."

This is not the whole of her sin. If that were all, I would not be tormented so much in the dark. When she was leaving the grove as if in a dream, her hand in the robber's, she suddenly turned pale, and pointed at me tied to the root of the cedar, and said, "Kill him! I cannot marry you as long as he lives." "Kill him!" she cried many times, as if she had gone crazy. Even now these words threaten to blow me headlong into the bottomless abyss of darkness. Has such a hateful thing come out of a human mouth ever before? Have such cursed words ever struck a human ear, even once? Even once such a . . . (A sudden cry of scorn.) At these words the robber himself turned pale. "Kill him!" she cried, clinging to his arms. Looking hard at her, he answered neither yes nor no. . . . But hardly had I thought about his answer before she had been knocked down into the bamboo leaves. (Again a cry of scorn.) Quietly folding his arms, he looked at me and said, "What would you like done with her? Kill her or save her? You have only to nod. Kill her?" For these words alone I would like to pardon his crime.

While I hesitated, she shrieked and ran into the depths of the grove. The robber instantly snatched at her, but he failed even to grasp her sleeve.

After she ran away, he took up my sword, and my bow and arrows. With a single stroke he cut one of my bonds. I remember his mumbling, "My fate is next." Then he disappeared from the grove. All was silent after that. No, I heard someone crying. Untying the rest of my bonds, I listened carefully, and noticed that it was my own crying. (Long silence.)

I raised my exhausted body from the root of the cedar. In front of me there was shining the small sword which my wife had dropped. I took it up and stabbed it into my breast. A bloody lump rose to my mouth, but I felt no pain. When my breast grew cold, everything was as silent as the dead in their graves. What profound silence! Not a single bird note was heard in the sky over this grave in the hollow of the mountains. Only a lonely light lingered on the cedars and the mountain. The light gradually grew fainter, till the cedars and bamboo were lost to view. Lying there, I was enveloped in deep silence.

Then someone crept up to me. I tried to see who it was. But darkness had already been gathering round me. Someone . . . that someone drew the small sword softly out of my breast in its invisible hand. At the same time blood again flowed into my mouth. And once and for all I sank down into the darkness of space.

Interpretation
and Background

Rashomon *as Modern Art*

by Parker Tyler

Rashomon, the Japanese film masterpiece, is a story about a double crime: rape and homicide (or possibly suicide). The time is the [twelfth] century A.D. It is told in retrospect, and in successive layers, by the three participants, the dead warrior (through a mediumistic priestess), his raped wife, and a notorious bandit perhaps responsible for the warrior's death as well as for his wife's violation, and by a woodcutter who alleges himself to have witnessed, accidentally, the whole episode. The quality of the film narrative is so fine that an astonishingly unified effect emerges from the conflicting stories furnished by the three principals and (following the inquest) by the lone witness. The bandit and the woman have separately fled the scene of the crimes, where the woodcutter claims, at first, to have arrived only in time to find the warrior's corpse. Nominally, the film comes under the familiar heading of stories that reconstruct crimes. However, this story does not go much beyond the presentation of each person's testimony.

The woman claims to have killed her husband in an irresponsible fit of horror after the rape took place; her husband claims to have committed hara-kiri out of grief and humiliation; the bandit claims to have killed him in honorable combat; and the woodcutter confirms the bandit's story while picturing the conduct of all participants quite differently from the ways they respectively describe it. As no trial of either of the living participants is shown, and as no consequent action reveals anything conclusive as to the crime, the decision as to the actual truth of the whole affair falls to the spectator's option. Since technically the woodcutter is the only "objective" witness, he might seem the most reliable of the four testifiers. But his integrity is *not* beyond question; the version by the warrior's ghost has contradicted his version in an important detail—one inadvertently confirmed by the woodcutter's implicit admission (in an incident following the inquest) that he stole a dagger at the scene of the crime. The ghost has testified that he felt "someone" draw from his breast the dagger with which he alleges he committed hara-kiri.

Logically, if one's aim be to establish in theory the "legal" truth of the affair, the only obvious method is to correlate all the admissible facts of the action with the four persons involved in order to determine their relative integrity as individuals—a procedure complicated necessarily not merely by the given criminal status of one participant but by the fact that all but the woodcutter have willingly assumed guilt. A further difficulty, in general, is that nothing of the background of any character is given beyond what can be assumed from his visible behavior and his social status; for example, there is only the merest hint of something unusual in the journey of the warrior and his lady through the forest. Again, even from direct observation, we have to depend a great deal on these persons as seen through the eyes of each other. So, unless one be prejudiced for one sex or another, one social class or another, it seems almost impossible to make a really plausible choice of the truth-teller (if any). Are we to conclude, in this dilemma, that *Rashomon* amounts to no more than a trick piece, a conventional mystery melodrama, left hanging? My answer is *No*. There are several things about the movie which argue it as unique and conscious art, the opposite of a puzzle; or at least, no more of a puzzle than those modern paintings of which a spectator may be heard to say: "But what is it? What is it supposed to mean?"

Perhaps more than one profane critic has wisecracked of a Picasso, a Dali, or an Ernst, that it demands, a posteriori, the method described by the police as "the reconstruction of the crime." My opinion is that the last thing required for the elucidation of *Rashomon*'s mystery is something corresponding to a jury's verdict. Such a judgment, aesthetically speaking, is as inutile for appreciating the substance of this movie as for approaching the art of Picasso. In *Rashomon,* there is no strategic effort to conceal any more than a modern painter's purpose is to conceal instead of reveal. The basic issue, in art, must always be *what* the creator desires to reveal. Of such a painting as Picasso's "Girl Before a Mirror," it may be said that it contains an "enigma." But this enigma is merely one specific aspect of the whole mystery of being, a particular insight into human consciousness in terms of the individual, and so has the complex poetry of which all profound art partakes. So with the enigma of *Rashomon.* This great Japanese film is a "mystery story" to the extent that existence itself is a mystery as conceived in the deepest psychological and aesthetic senses. As applied to a movie of this class, however, such a theory is certainly unfamiliar and therefore has to be explained.

Chagall with his levitated fantasy world and childhood symbols, Picasso with his creative analysis of psychological movements translated into pictorial vision—such painters set forth *nude* mysteries of human experience; each, in the static field of the painting, reveals multiple aspects of a single reality, whether literally or in symbols. *Rashomon,* as a time art, cinema, corresponds with multiple-image painting as a space art. The simplest rendering of time phases in an object within the unilateral space of a single picture is, of course, in Futurist painting, such as Balla's famous dog, ambling by the moving skirts of its owner; the dachshund's legs are portrayed multiply with a fanlike, flickering kind of image similar to images as seen in the old-fashioned "bioscope" movie machine. The same dynamic principle was illustrated by Muybridge's original time-photography of a running horse, except that the register there was not instantaneous but successive; at least, the photographer had the cinematic idea of keeping pace with a running horse to show the pendulum-like span of its front and hind legs while its body seemed to stay in the same place (treadmill dynamics). Even in the contemporary movie camera, some movements may be so fast that one gets the sort of blur shown in Futurist images. The analogy of *Rashomon* with such procedures of stating physical movement is that, for the single action photographed, a complex action (or "episode") is substituted, and for the single viewpoint toward this action, multiple (and successive) viewpoints. The camera in this movie is actually trained four times on what theoretically is the same episode; if the results are different each time, it is because each time the camera represents the viewpoint of a different person; a viewpoint mainly different, of course, not because of the physical angle (the camera is never meant to substitute for subjective vision) but because of the psychological angle.

"Simultaneous montage" in cinema is the double exposure of two views so that multiple actions occur in a *unilateral space visually* while existing in *separate spaces literally* and possibly—as when a person and his visual recollection are superimposed on the same film frame—also in separate times. A remarkable aspect of the method of depicting memory in *Rashomon* is its simplicity: each person, squatting in Japanese fashion as he testifies, squarely faces the camera and speaks; then, rather than simultaneous montage, a flashback takes place: the scene shifts wholly to the fatal spot in the forest. The police magistrate is never shown and no questions addressed to the witnesses are heard. When it is the dead man's turn to testify, the priestess performs the required rite, becomes possessed by his spirit, speaks in his voice, and the scene shifts back as in the other cases. Thus we receive the successive versions of the action with little intervention between them and with the minimum of "courtroom action."

Of course, there is a framing story, which retrospectively reveals the inquest itself. The action literally begins at the gate, Rashomon, a great ruin where the woodcutter and the priest, who have previously seen the woman and been present at the inquest, are sheltered during a rainstorm; joined by a tramp, these two gradually reveal everything that has taken place according to the several versions. What is important is the inherent value of the way the technique of the flashback has been variously used. The separate stories are equally straightforward, equally forceful; no matter which version is being related, his own or another's, every participant behaves with the same conviction. As a result (it was certainly this spectator's experience) one is compelled to believe each story implicitly as it unfolds, and oddly none seems to cancel another out. Therefore it would be only from the policeman's viewpoint of wanting to pin guilt on one of the persons that, ultimately, any obligation would be felt to sift the conflicting evidence and render a formal verdict. Despite the incidental category of its form, *Rashomon* as a work of art naturally seems to call for a response having nothing to do with a courtroom.

Of an event less significant, less stark and rudimentary in terms of human behavior, the technical question of "the truth" might prove insistent enough to embarrass one's judgment. The inevitable impulse, at first sight, is to speculate on which of those who claim guilt is really guilty of the warrior's death. But whatever conclusion be tentatively reached, what eventually slips back into the spectator's mind, and possesses it, is the traumatic violence of the basic pattern: that violence which is the heart of the enigma. The civilization of this medieval period is turned topsy-turvy by the bandit's strategy, in which he tricks the man, ties him up, and forces him to witness his wife's violation. It is only from this point forward that the stories differ: the woman's reaction to the bandit's assault, the husband's behavior after being freed from his bonds—everything is disputed by one version or another. But is not the heart of the confusion *within the event itself*? Is this happening not one so frightfully destructive of human poise and ethical custom that it breeds its own ambiguity, and that this ambiguity infects the minds of these people?

All the participants are suffering from shock: the warrior's agonized ghost, his hysterical wife, the bandit, when caught, seized with mad bravado. Unexpectedly—for the paths of the couple and the bandit have crossed purely by accident—three lives have been irretrievably altered after being reduced to the most primitive condition conceivable. Two men (in a manner in which, at best, etiquette has only a vestigial role) have risked death for the possession of a woman. Basically, it is a pattern that was born with the beginnings of mankind. Such an event, in civilized times of high culture, would of itself contain something opaque and even incredible. What matters morally is not how, from moment to moment, the affair was played out by its actors but that it should have been played *at all*. The illicit impulse springing up in the bandit's breast as the lady's long veil blows aside, is so violent that its consequences attack the sense of reality at its moral root. Regardless of what literally took place in the forest's depths that mild summer day, each participant is justified in reconstructing it in a manner to redeem the prestige of the moral sense, which, consciously or not, is a civilized person's most precious possession. It should be emphasized that it is the Japanese people who are involved, and that to them honor is of peculiarly paramount value; even the bandit is quick to seize the opportunity to maintain— truthfully or not—that he behaved like a man of caste rather than an outlaw; he has testified that following the rape (to which, he says, the woman yielded willingly) he untied the husband and worsted him in fair swordplay.

Hence, a psychologically unilateral, indisputable perspective exists in which the tragic episode can be viewed *by the spectator;* a perspective contrary to that in which one of the persons appears technically guilty of the warrior's death. This perspective is simply the catastrophe as a single movement which temporarily annihilated the moral reality on which civilized human consciousness is based. The "legal" or objective reality of the affair (what might be called its *statistics*) is exactly what cannot be recovered because the physical episode, as human action, has been *self-annihilating.* Of course, then, it might be claimed that the woodcutter, not being involved except as a spectator, is a disinterested witness of the episode, and accordingly his story that the three actors in the tragedy really played a grim farce, in which two cowards were the heroes and a shrew the heroine, is the correct version. But the opening scene of the framing story makes it plain that the woodcutter's mind is in a state similar to that of the participants themselves; indeed, he is evidently dismayed and apparently by the fact that all their testimony belies what he proceeds to reveal to the priest and the tramp as "the truth." However, as the shocked witness of such a debacle of the social order—in any case a victory of evil over good— this peasant may have withheld his testimony out of superstitious timidity. If, in fact, he saw all that took place, then the added confusion that the participants contradict each other may raise bewilderment in his simple mind—may even tempt him to exploit his subconscious envy and resentment against his betters by imagining their behavior as disgraceful and ludicrous. It seems within *Rashomon*'s subtle pattern to suggest that even a simple, disinterested witness should be drawn psychologically into the chaos of this incident; after all, there is no proof that he did not invent his own account in competition with the others'. This assumption would lend credit to the conclusion that the real function of each witness's story is to salvage his own sense of reality, however close his version to the event as it took place. Perhaps it would be accurate to add that the facts themselves have no true legal status since each witness is forced to draw on his subjective imagination rather than on his capacity to observe. In this case, each is in the position of the proto-artist, who uses reality only as a crude norm; the sense of invention enters *into* reality. On the other hand, there is the literal truth of the denouement, the climax of the framing story, in which the woodcutter adopts a foundling baby who has been left in the gate's interior. The relation of this incident to the story proper strikes me as the most problematical element of all, if only because the film would have remained intact without it.

Morally, of course, this incident functions as a reinstatement of human values in the sense of good. But the specifically religious view that humanity has hopelessly degraded itself in the forest episode (the view represented by the priest) is more external than essential to the whole conception. The priest thinks in terms equivalent, logically, to the law's terms: truth or falsehood. Since some lying is self-evident, the sin of concealment is added to crime; *i.e.,* concealment of the truth, not of the crime, for all profess crime. Ironically enough, *confession* has become a sin. What seems significant to the whole is the collective nature of the liars: they literally outnumber the truth-teller (whichever he may be). The "sin" involved has gone beyond individual performance and exists objectively as would a natural cataclysm such as a volcanic eruption. That each participant assumes guilt, including the dead man, reveals the comprehensiveness and irresistibility of the disorder. A lie, then, actually becomes the symbol of the operation by which these people mutually regain their moral identities. These identities having been destroyed as though by an objective force beyond anyone's control, any means seems fair to regain them. Since, however, they cannot separate themselves from the sense of *tragedy,* they prefer to be tragedy's heroes—its animating will rather than its passive objects. But why should the three tragedies seem as one?

To revert to our analogy with the visual media of painting and still photography, the plastic reality with which we have to deal in *Rashomon* is multiform rather than uniform. Within one span of time-and-space, reality (the episode in the forest) has been disintegrated. While the witnesses' stories accomplish its reintegration, they do not do so in terms of the *physically unilateral* except in the final aesthetic sense in which the totality of a work exists all at once in a spectator's mind. The analogy is complex, but literally it is with the Futuristic image of the walking dog; like this image, the total of *Rashomon* varies only in detail and degree. There is no variation on the background and origin of the tragedy; no contradiction as to the main physical patterns of the rape and the death of the warrior by a blade wound. So the main visual aspect is held firmly, unilaterally, in place. Another image of Futurist painting renders the angles of air displacement caused by the nose of a racing auto. Such "displacements" exist in *Rashomon* severally in the respective accounts of a physical action deriving from one main impetus: the desire to possess a woman.

Picasso, Pablo. Girl Before a Mirror. *March, 1932. Oil on canvas 63¾" x 51¼". Collection The Museum of Modern Art, New York. Gift of Mrs. Simon Guggenheim.*

Dr. Schapiro's analysis of the Picasso painting was expounded during "A Life Round Table on Modern Art," excerpts from which appeared in Life, *October 11, 1948.*

The total psychological space in this movie, because of its complexity, is rendered in literal time as is music. A similar psychological space is rendered *simultaneously* in Picasso's "Girl Before a Mirror" by the device of the mirror as well as by the double image of profile-and-fullface on the girl. Her moonlike face has a symbolic integralness as different "phases" of the same person; that is, her fullface denotes her personality as it confronts the world and her profile her personality as it confronts itself: the mirror image in which the fullface character of her aspect is diminished. To Meyer Schapiro we owe a basic observation as to this painting: it plays specifically on the body image which each individual has of himself and others, and which is distinct from the anatomical image peculiarly available to photography. The mirror image in Picasso's work thus asserts a psychological datum parallel with the dominantly subjective testimony of each witness in *Rashomon*'s tragedy. The mirror of the movie screen is like the mirror in the painting as telescoped within the image of the total painting; successively, we see people as they think of themselves and as they are to others; for example, at one point during the woman's story, the camera substitutes for the viewpoint of her husband toward whom she lifts a dagger: we see her as conceived by herself but also as she would have been in her husband's eyes. In revealing, with such expressiveness and conviction, what novels have often revealed through first-person narratives or the interior monologue, the film necessarily emphasizes its *visual* significance. The sum of these narratives in *Rashomon* rests on the elements of the tragedy in which all agree: one raped, one was raped, one killed, one was killed. The "variations" are accountable through something which I would place parallel with Schapiro's body-image concept: the *psychic image* that would apply especially to the memory of a past event in which the body image is charged with maintaining, above all, its moral integrity, its ideal dignity. In a sense, Picasso's girl reconstructs and synthesizes her outer self-division within the depths of the mirror; so in the depths of each person's memory, in *Rashomon,* is re-created the image of what took place far away in the forest as consistent with his ideal image of himself.

In modern times, the human personality—as outstandingly demonstrated in the tragi-comedies of Pirandello—is easily divided against itself. But what makes a technically schizophrenic situation important and dramatically interesting is, paradoxically, the individual's sense of his former or possible unity, for without this sense he would not struggle morally against division: he would be satisfied to be "more than one person." In analytical cubism, we have a pictorial style expressing an ironic situation within the human individual's total physique, including his clothes; we do not perceive, within an individual portrayed by Picasso in this manner, a moral "split" or psychological "confusion"; rather we see the subject's phenomenal appearance portrayed formalistically in terms of its internal or "depth" elements, its overlaid facets, or complex layers of being, which—though presumably not meant to signify a conflict in the personality—correspond logically, nevertheless, to the moral dialectic within all consciousness (subjective/objective, personal/social, and so on). The same logical correspondence is seen even more plainly in the anatomical dialectic of Tchelitchew's recent paintings, where the separate inner systems are seen in labyrinthine relation to the skin surface. Indeed, man as an internal labyrinth is common to diverse styles of modern painting, all such styles necessarily implying, as human statements, the sometimes bewildering complexity of man's spiritual being. Great beauty is justifiably found in such aesthetic forms, which indirectly symbolize an ultimate mystery: that *human* mystery to which *Rashomon* so eloquently testifies in its own way and which comprises the transition from birth to death, from the organic to the inorganic, which is the individual's necessary material fate.

Against the awareness of his material fate, the individual erects many defenses: art, pleasure, ethics, God, religion, immortality—ideas, sensations, and acts whose continuity in him are preserved by constant cultivation, periodic renewal, unconscious "testimony." These constitute his moral identity in the social order. In them resides the essence of his being, the law of his contentment (such as it be), and his rational ability to function from hour to hour. In the lives of the persons of *Rashomon,* where this objective order prevailed, utter chaos was suddenly injected. Each person was shaken out of himself, became part of that blind flux which joins the intuition of the suspense-before-birth with that of the suspense-before-death and whose name is terror. This was largely because of the tragedy's physical violence, which temporarily vanquished human reason. If we look at the terror of war as depicted in Picasso's "Guernica," we observe a social cataclysm of which the forest episode in *Rashomon* is a microcosm. Curiously enough, "Guernica" happens to be divided vertically into four main sections, or panels, which Picasso has subtly unified by overlapping certain formal elements. Thus, while the great massacre is of course highly simplified here in visual terms, it is moreover synthesized by means of four stages or views. As wrenched by violence as are the individual forms, they congregate, so to speak, to make order out of confusion. Though Picasso was not recomposing from memory, he might have been; in any case, the drive of art is toward formal order and the individuals in *Rashomon,* as proto-artists, have this same drive. As gradually accumulated, the sum total of *Rashomon* constitutes a *time mural* whose unity lies in the fact that, however different are the imaginations of the four witnesses, whatever harsh vibrations their mutual contradictions set up, the general design (as the filmmakers have molded it) remains and dominates the work's final aspect of great beauty and great truth.

Memory of Defeat in Japan:
A Reappraisal of Rashomon

by James F. Davidson

As a particular insight into Japanese feelings, it is worth taking another look at the most widely acclaimed of Japan's dramatic products since the war, the origin of which dates well back into the [Allied] occupation [of Japan]. It is now more than two years since the film *Rashomon* was first seen by New York audiences after having won the grand prize at the Venice Film Festival. It was subsequently shown in many American cities and won critics' citations as an outstanding foreign film. The purpose of this review is to point out some implications of *Rashomon* in terms of the Japanese reflection on their defeat and occupation which were completely overlooked by American reviews at the time. These overtones are present throughout the picture and come through strongly in many of its details. Without producing a consistent theme, they heighten the dramatic effect of the story upon a Japanese audience in a way which is easily lost upon the foreign observer.

The story is laid in the ancient capital of Kyoto, during a troubled period in the [twelfth] century. It concerns a samurai and his wife waylaid on the road by a notorious bandit. The man is killed and the woman flees, later seeking refuge in a temple whence she is

This article was written shortly after the signing of the military-aid pact between Japan and the United States in 1954. In it, the author, who was a member of the secretariat of the Far Eastern Commission and worked for the Department of State, seeks to arrive at a new understanding of a country that had been a subdued enemy but had now become an ally. Reprinted, by permission, from *The Antioch Review*, Vol. XIV, No. 4 (December, 1954).

brought to the police magistrate after the capture of the bandit. A woodcutter who found the body and a Buddhist priest who passed the couple on the day of the crime are present at the testimony. As the picture opens, these two relate the events to a stranger while the three seek shelter from the rain in the ruins of the great gate of Kyoto, the Rashomon.

The bandit, Tajomaru, boasted that he had slain the man. Catching a glimpse of the woman as the couple passed him on the road, he had resolved to possess her and, if possible, to do so without killing her husband. With a tale of swords and mirrors buried near an abandoned temple, he enticed the man into the woods where he overcame and bound him. On being led to the spot, the wife attacked the bandit with a dagger, fighting like a tigress until at last, exhausted and hysterical, she not only succumbed but finally returned his embrace.

Afterwards, as he was about to leave, she stopped him, saying that she could not stand disgrace in the eyes of two men. One must die, and she belong to the other. He released the husband and they fought. After the samurai had won the bandit's admiration by crossing swords with him longer than any previous foe, he was slain. Finding the woman gone, the bandit took the horse and weapons, except for the dagger, which he forgot. He was apprehended shortly after, writhing ignominiously with stomach cramps as a result of drinking from a polluted stream.

According to the wife, the bandit left after the attack, laughing derisively. She ran to her husband to find nothing but contempt in his eyes, even when she cut his ropes and begged him to kill her. Maddened by his stare, she approached with the dagger, fainted, and recovered to find that she had plunged it into his chest.

Next, in a procedure which modern homicide squads must contemplate wistfully, the testimony of the dead man is obtained through a medium. He says that the bandit urged his wife to go with him, declaring his love and saying that her husband would not want her now. To his horror, she not only consented, but as they left she pulled the bandit back and cried, "Kill him!" The bandit stared at her in unbelief and then said to her husband, "What do you want me to do with this woman? Kill her? Spare her? Just nod if you agree." For that, says the dead man, he could almost forgive him. As he hesitated, she wrenched free and fled. After a chase, the bandit returned alone, cut his ropes and left. He rose, sobbing, found the dagger and killed himself. As he lost consciousness, he was aware of someone approaching and drawing out the dagger.

At this point in the film, the stranger laughs at the discomfort of the two narrators. The priest is miserable because the same faith that requires him to believe the dead man's story is shaken by the account of the woman's treachery. The woodcutter suddenly bursts out that he knows the man was killed with a sword because he saw it happen. He concealed his knowledge from the police out of a desire not to be involved. Coming upon the clearing, he had seen the man bound and the bandit entreating the woman. Finally, she ran to her husband, cut his ropes, and threw herself on the ground halfway between the men. The bandit drew, but the husband refused to risk his life for her, saying, "I regret the loss of my horse much more . . ." The bandit considered a moment, then turned to leave and rebuffed the woman as she ran after him.

She began to laugh wildly and denounced both of them. She had long been sick of "this farce," indicating her husband, and had been thrilled to learn the identity of her attacker. Perhaps Tajomaru was a way out for her. But no! He did not take her like a conqueror. She told her husband that he could hardly sneer at her honor if he was too poor a specimen to fight for her. Goaded by her, they fought unwillingly, unskillfully, even cravenly. It was not a duel; it was a terrified brawl.

At last the husband was trapped in the undergrowth and, shouting that he did not want to die, was run through. The staggering, panting Tajomaru returned to the woman, who had watched in horrified fascination. She fought him off and fled. He then gathered up both swords and left.

When the woodcutter has finished his account, the stranger again laughs at the unhappiness of the other two over this exposure of human frailty and deceit. "Everyone wants to forget unpleasant things, so they make up stories," he has said earlier. These three now become principals in the epilogue, which is very important to an understanding of the film. They hear a cry and discover an abandoned baby around a corner of the gate. The stranger, who reaches it first, strips the blankets from it. The horrified priest takes the baby while the woodcutter seizes the stranger and denounces him as the incarnation of evil. He justifies himself, saying that the parents have abandoned their duty and he is not obliged to take it up. Everyone must live any way he can, and if he does not steal the blankets someone else will. Still pressed by the woodcutter, he rebounds with the taunt that he knows why the last story was concealed from the police. He accuses the woodcutter of having taken the dagger, described by the bandit as valuable, from the scene of the crime. The crestfallen woodcutter makes no denial, and the stranger dashes off into the rain with the blankets, jeering.

The two stand in silence. Then the woodcutter takes the child, saying that he has six and one more will make little difference. The priest thanks him for restoring his faith in man and, as the sky clears, watches him proceed homeward from the steps of the gate.

Not all American critics were favorably impressed with *Rashomon*. Even reviews that praised it contained adjectives such as "slow," "repetitious," "humorlessly solemn," and "confused." The extravagance of the acting was much remarked. Two reviewers, from their mutually distant corners in *Time* and the *New Republic,* singled out the sentimental epilogue as a serious flaw, arbitrarily and unfitly added. It was duly noted that the film draws from the works of the brilliant author Ryunosuke Akutagawa who committed suicide in 1927 at the age of thirty-five. The basis, however, was not a novel as widely reported, but two short stories. The stories are completely separate, and the scenarist-director, Akira Kurosawa, combined them into a product considerably different from either. The original stories therefore throw some light on the central problem of the film.

The first story, "Yabu no naka" ("In a Grove"), supplied the basic plot: the conflicting accounts of the same crime by those involved. Akutagawa took an old melodrama and, with the clever detachment for which he is famous, made it ask Pilate's question. The circumstances presented as actual are essentially the same as in the film. Then there are the confessions of the bandit, the wife, and the dead man. That is all. There is no fourth account by an eyewitness, no comment on the implications of the testimonies.

The second story, "Rashomon," in addition to the title, contributed the setting, atmosphere, and the idea of characters who discuss right and wrong, duty and necessity. . . . Why was an atmosphere of gloom and decay, of physical and spiritual misery, chosen as a background in the film? The original story of the crime contains no such atmosphere, no linking of the event to the conditions of the times. Its effect is all the more striking because of this. If the sole aim of the film was to depict individual lust, selfishness, and falsehood as a timeless problem, as favorable American reviews acclaimed, then it could well have been more faithful to the spirit, as well as the words, of Akutagawa in developing the remarkable event in less remarkable circumstances. It should not be forgotten that this film was made in the first instance for Japanese audiences, at a time when Japanese films were only beginning to emerge from an understandable period of complete escapism. A drama laid in medieval Japan, involving questions of human nature, could have provided a respectable type of escape without sacrificing its integrity. Yet the picture opens on the ruined Rashomon: once the great architectural symbol of the capital of Japan, now the crumbling reflection of a devastated city whence the seat of power has moved. It is deluged by a relentless, windless rain. Under the gate sit the priest and the woodcutter, exchanging mute glances and headshakes. The priest slowly recites the kinds of disaster that have befallen. "Yet . . . even I have never heard anything as horrible as this before." It becomes clear that he is in danger of losing his faith. Later, shrugging off their story, the stranger says, "After all, who's honest nowadays?" It is hard to believe that a Japanese audience was not being led to refer to their own experience and to see the events of the story accordingly.

The man and wife are depicted at the outset as the very embodiment of Japanese virtue, refinement, and prosperity. He is a samurai, of the ancient warrior caste whose tradition was so carefully preserved until 1945; handsome, weaponed, and well-dressed. As they pass the priest, he turns and laughs happily up at his wife. She is mounted on a fine horse and veiled from view. Lovely and petite, she seemed to the bandit in that first glance, he says, like an angel.

The bandit, as portrayed in the film, is a most remarkable character. In the original story, he wears a blue silk kimono and joins the couple as a traveling companion in order to divert them from the road with talk of buried treasure. There is evidently nothing unusual in his appearance or manner, and he easily disguises his identity and intentions so as to be accept-

Toshiro Mifune as the bandit (Daiei publicity still).

able. The film Tajomaru, on the other hand, is a half-clad savage, uncouth, insolent, and raucous, who "capers about the screen," as the London *Times* said, "like a ferocious, demented Puck bellowing with maniacal laughter." He appears the least Japanese of all the characters, and a sort of incarnation of the *oni*, or ogre, of Japanese folklore, which has often been interpreted as a representation of the foreigner. His build and movements, even his features, suggest something of the gangling awkwardness that appears in

Japanese caricatures of Occidentals. He is alternately terrifying and ridiculous, but always alien to the others. This serves to emphasize the avariciousness and foolishness of the samurai, who, significantly, leaves his wife and undertakes the journey to his ruin as a commercial venture.

Details from "The Black Ship Scroll," by an anonymous Japanese eyewitness of the day-to-day meetings between the Japanese and the Americans who arrived at the fishing port of Shimoda in April, 1854, in "black ships" under the command of Commodore Perry. Left: The scroll's commentary reads, in part: "Picture of American sailors dancing about under the influence of strong drink." Right: "True Portrait of Perry, Envoy of the Republic of North America. His age is

The scene in which the wife is overcome in a prolonged kiss (in itself still a shocker for Japanese audiences) is more horrifying because her attacker is a sweating, scratching, bug-slapping barbarian than it would have been with Akutagawa's blue-kimonoed outlaw. The strong suggestion of cultural difference, verg-

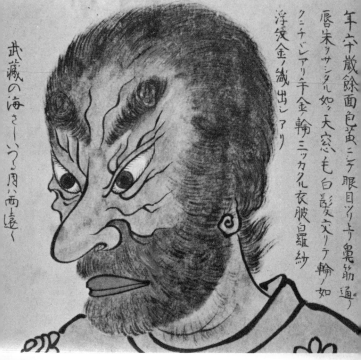

over 60. His face is sallow, eyes slanted, nose prominent. His lips are as though rouged." More folklore than portrait, *this detail shows, not what Perry looked like, but what a hairy foreigner was alleged to look like.*

Reproduced by permission of The Japan Society of San Francisco, from Oliver Statler's The Black Ship Scroll, *with scroll commentary translated by Richard Lane (Rutland, Vermont: Charles E. Tuttle Co., 1963).*

ing on the ethnic, gives her ultimate lustful response an additional meaning. The problem is as old as conquest. And the epilogue of the abandoned child takes on a practical significance which removes from it much of the stigma of artistic error which it must bear if considered only as a disconnected attempt to restore faith in goodness.

In the original story, the wife tells her husband very simply that she cannot live with her disgrace and his contempt, and that she cannot leave him alive as a witness to them. Then she kills him, but fails in her attempt to kill herself. In the film, her confession is, in effect, a plea of temporary insanity. While she does not admit to any guilt in yielding to the bandit, nothing is done to remove the impression made by the scene which shows her to the audience as finally sharing his passion. She sobs hysterically and concludes her story by beseeching the audience—which sits in the position of the judge throughout the testimonies—"What should a poor helpless woman like me do?"

The woodcutter, in the original story simply a witness who found the body, becomes an eyewitness whose account provides a devastating contrast to the others. Yet in the end he, too, is implicated, and the truth again eludes the others. Aside from his story, he has a place in the commentary and the epilogue as one of the only two commoners in the picture. The other is the stranger, who accepts human depravity with a laugh, jeers at the struggles of those who would deny it, and makes what he can for himself without scruple. The woodcutter is a simple man, striving to be honest under the burden of a large family and hard times. He is disturbed by a sense of his own guilt and the knowledge of the guilt of the other three. The priest, with less knowledge of the event than the other, shares his feeling with even greater unhappiness, for he perceives its fatal consequences for his faith.

The [London] *Times,* more perspicacious in its perplexity over *Rashomon* than the American accolades, notes that there is little ritual about it and that even the music does not seem to be distinctively Japanese. This touches an important point about the epilogue. The picture has been filled with noise and confusion. Aside from the hysterics of the woman, much of the noise has been the derisive laughter of the bandit and the cynical stranger: the laughter which, even in silence, rings in the ears of a proud man defeated and reduced. There is practically no ritual and all reminders of contemporary Japan are unpleasant. Then, as the woodcutter takes the baby from the priest and goes home, both bow twice, ceremoniously. The priest stands on the steps of the Rashomon, which no longer looks so ruined in the emerging sunlight. The music has suddenly become traditional. The final act of grace has restored a particularly Japanese kind of rightness.

There is a striking similarity with a final scene in *The Well-Digger's Daughter*, where the unmarried mother, the repentant father, and the grandparents, separated by social barriers, are united around the crib of the baby. Raimu, as the well-digger, has a speech in which he urges that the past be forgotten in love for the child. "For here," he says, "is our hope. Here is France." The French in 1946 had need of a hope in which to sink the bitter divisions of the past. Postwar Japan is in need of a belief on which to found a duty. Surely the epilogue of *Rashomon* points, after the unanswerable questions raised in the story, to a basic belief and duty for Japanese to hold to. The old vision of a hopeful future springing from a glorious past is lost, and the way to its recovery lies through a maze of doubtful thoughts about misfortune, guilt, and shame. Yet there is a new Japan, which demands love and care, like the abandoned child, not because of its auspicious or legitimate beginnings, but because it is alive and will perish without them.

It would be foolish to argue that the film is a complete or consistent allegory. To refer again to the *Times* review, however, ". . . something, some part of a country's habits of thinking, some perhaps unconscious reflection of its prejudices, and preferences, filters through the lens of the camera to perplex or amuse the foreigner." Much of the perplexity can be avoided by recognizing the implications for the Japanese audience, intermediate between the basic story and the more universal meaning. These aid the story in supporting the commentary, and fill the picture in spots that would otherwise be empty. They also help to account for the unrestrained, un-Oriental acting. The actors are portraying emotions which Japanese are conditioned by recent events to feel strongly, and their portrayals must be adequate to these feelings as well as to the events of the story. In these terms, even the agonized contortions of the medium as she establishes contact with the spirit of the dead samurai seem to have some meaning.

Rashomon was not popular in Japan on its first showing, although there has been more interest in a second circulation since its international awards. It is not a popular-type production, but many circles there have received it enthusiastically. Without substantiating the specific arguments of this review, a prominent Japanese official assured the writer that the significance for the current situation in Japan was widely accepted. Any full understanding of the film, he added, must consider it in terms of the current feelings of the Japanese.

The story told by each of the three participants protects his self-respect. In the account of the woodcutter, the common man, they are all revealed as frauds. The fight is a travesty on that described by the bandit, after which the mighty Tajomaru, heaving with fright and exertion, goes off to be betrayed into capture by a rebellion of his own innards. Bitter satire on the heroic virtues finds a natural response in a defeated nation. Still, we are reminded, the woodcutter also has a motive for changing the facts to conceal his guilt.

How did the old beliefs and loyalties die? Did they perish in a defeat at arms which "liberated" those who had already begun to see through them? Did they, in a manner of speaking, annihilate themselves in shame and sorrow for a people no longer worthy of them? Were they destroyed by those who held them dear because they were an unbearable reminder of duties that could no longer be fulfilled? Or were they done in, in an uncertain scuffle of ideals and proclamations and conflicting directives that left nothing firm and whole in their place? Finally, since ideas do not die as men die, the question remains, are they really dead? It seems unlikely that thoughtful Japanese would see *Rashomon* without having some of these questions brought to mind. Even small touches may strike a chord. For example, when the bandit pleads with the woman to go with him and then, impatient at getting no reply, shakes her roughly and shouts, "Answer. Tell me you'll be my wife," some might see something of the ambivalent attitude of SCAP [Supreme Commander for the Allied Powers, *i.e.,* General Douglas MacArthur].

Just how intentionally Kurosawa worked these overtones into his film is questionable. Since he has taught us so well that the confession of a principal may be a poor guide to truth, perhaps we shall never know. . . . If the implications for Japanese are those here described, they carry little self-pity and have the same objective balancing of error and guilt into an open question as the rest of the film. This is what makes the solution of the epilogue particularly touching. As an artistic achievement and as a searching of the soul, *Rashomon* is something of which any country could be proud.

Rashomon *and Kurosawa*

by Donald Richie

Kurosawa had for some time wanted to make the film that eventually became *Rashomon.* A scenario was written, a budget was determined, and then (in 1948) the picture was cancelled because the small Toyoko Company, which was to have financed it, decided it was too much of a risk. Toho—Kurosawa's company off and on for a number of years—was against it. Then Daiei signed a one-year distribution and production contract with Kurosawa. He and his associates left Toho to form the short-lived Motion Picture Art Association, and one of the director's hopes was to be able to make this picture.

After making *Scandal,* Kurosawa showed Daiei the script which became *Rashomon.* "It was a bit too short . . . but all of my friends liked it very much. Daiei, however, did not understand it and kept asking: But what is it about? I made it longer, put on a beginning and an ending—and they eventually agreed to make it. Thus Daiei joined those—Shochiku for *The Idiot,* Toho for *Record of a Living Being* [released in the United States as *I Live in Fear*]—who were brave enough to try something different." This is a very charitable statement. Actually Daiei was adamant in its refusal to understand. Masaichi Nagata, head of the studio and standing somewhat in relation to Japanese film as Darryl Zanuck once stood to American production, walked out on the first screening and, until the picture began winning prizes abroad, was very fond of telling the press how little he understood *his* film—his, since he, in the manner of a Goldwyn or a Zanuck or a Wald, often signs his own name as executive producer. Toho never gave adequate foreign distribution to *Record of a Living Being* and Shochiku butchered *The Idiot.*

Source

The beginnings of *Rashomon* lie in the stories of that brilliant and erratic stylist Ryunosuke Akutagawa. His position in Japanese letters, though secure, has always been special—as special as that of Poe in America or Maupassant in France. He has always been extremely popular and also critically well-thought-of, almost despite his popularity. Yet he has never been considered in the mainstream of Japanese literature. His defenders point to his inventive style: his detractors call him "Western" in his orientation. He *is* "Western" in the same way as Kurosawa: he is concerned with truths which are ordinarily outside pragmatic Japanese morality and, being concerned with them, he questions them. This he does with an involuted, elliptical style, the essence of which is irony. In translation he sounds very *fin de siècle,* a better Beardsley, a less involved Lafcadio Hearn—though there is no trace of this in Kurosawa's film.

Akutagawa is content to question all moral values, all truth. Kurosawa is not. Neither anarchist nor misanthrope, he insists upon hope, upon the possibility of a freedom of choice. Like the priest in *Rashomon,* he cannot believe that men are evil—and, indeed, if Kurosawa has a spokesman in the film it is probably the priest, who is ultimately trusting.

The Story

There is, however, much more to the film than this. There is an apparent mystery, an elliptical intent, which has fascinated audiences all over the world. Daiei was quite right to ask what the picture was about, though its dismissal of the film as being a kind of mystification was ill-judged. One of the most fascinating aspects of the film is just that it is extremely difficult to determine *what* it means. . . .

One doubts very much that Kurosawa was deeply interested in objective truth in this or in any other film. This is because the *why* is always implied. And in none of his pictures is Kurosawa even slightly interested in the why of a matter. Instead, always, *how.* This offers a clue. The level of objective truth is not the truly interesting one. Much more interesting is the level of subjective truth. If the truth searched for becomes subjective, then no one lies, and the stories are wildly at variance.

Truth as it appears to others. This is one of the themes, perhaps the main one of this picture. No one lied. They all told the story the way they saw it, the way they believed it, and they all told the truth. Kurosawa therefore does not question truth. He questions reality.

Once asked why he thought that *Rashomon* had become so popular, both in Japan and abroad, he answered: "Well, you see . . . it's about this rape." Everyone laughed but the answer is not, perhaps, so cynical as it sounds. *Rashomon* is *about* an action as few pictures are *about* anything at all. We can turn the object this way and that, look at it from various angles, and it resembles a number of things but *is* only one thing, the object that it is. The film is about a rape (and a murder) but, more than this, it is about the reality of these events. Precisely, it is about what five people [bandit, samurai, wife, woodcutter, and priest] think this reality consists of. How a thing happens may reflect nothing about the thing itself, but it must reflect something about the person involved in the happening and supplying the how.

Five people interpret an action and each interpretation is different because, in the telling and in the retelling, the people reveal not the action but themselves. This is why Kurosawa could leave the plot, insofar as there is one, dangling and unresolved. The fact that it *is* unresolved is itself one of the meanings of the film.

In all of Kurosawa's pictures there is this preoccupation with the conflict between illusion (the reactions of the five) and reality (the fact of the rape and murder). To do something is to realize that it is far different from what one had thought. To have done something and then to explain it completes the cycle because this too is (equally) different from what the thing itself was. Given a traumatic experience, one fraught with emotional connotations (murder, rape), reality escapes even more swiftly.

One can now assign various reasons for the five having seen and heard the things that they thought they saw and heard. All the stories have in common one single element—pride. Tajomaru is proud to have raped and fought and killed; the wife is proud to have (perhaps) killed; the dead husband is proud to have killed himself; and the woodcutter is proud to have seen and robbed. They are proud of these actions and we know because they insist upon them. One confesses only what one is openly or secretly proud of, which is the reason that contrition is rarely sincere. But the reasons for the pride, as Parker Tyler has indicated in his fine analysis of this film, are not those commonly encountered.

Each is proud of what he did because, as he might tell you: "It is just the sort of thing that I would do." Each thinks of his character as being fully formed, of being a *thing*, like the rape or the dagger is a thing, and of his therefore (during an emergency such as this) being capable of only a certain number of (consistent) reactions. They are *in character* because they have defined their own character for themselves and will admit none of the surprising opportunities which must occur when one does not. They "had no choice"; circumstances "forced" their various actions; what each did "could not be helped." It is no wonder that the reported actions refuse to agree with each other. As the commoner has wisely remarked: "Men are only men . . . they can't tell the truth, not even to themselves." One of the points of the picture then is not that men will not but that men *can* not tell the truth. The priest sees this: "It is because men are so weak. That's why they lie. That's why they must deceive themselves."

If one is going to agree that one is a certain kind of person one also agrees that one is engaged in self-deception, in bad faith. We know what Kurosawa thinks about this. From *Sanshiro Sugata* on, his villains have been in bad faith, that is, they see themselves as a kind of person to whom only certain actions, certain alternatives are open. In the effort to create themselves they only codify; in the effort to free themselves (by making action simpler and therefore easier) they limit themselves.

It is interesting that *Rashomon* should have been a historical film—Kurosawa's second (since the Japanese tend to think of the Meiji period—the era of *Sanshiro Sugata*—as being somehow modern), because this limitation of spirit, this tacit agreement (social in its scope) that one *is* and cannot *become,* is one feudalistic precept which plagues the country to this day. This was as useful to the Kamakura Government as it proved to be to the administration during the last war. In *Rashomon,* as in *The Men Who Tread on the Tiger's Tail* and *Sanjuro,* Kurosawa is presenting an indictment of feudal remains. That he sets the scene in the Heian period [794–1185] is merely due to Akutagawa's having used it, and where the director follows the author in this film, he does so literally. The people, and their way of thinking, are—twelfth century or present day—completely feudal. It is as though in this film he is holding up a mirror.

In more ways than one. *Rashomon* is like a vast distorting mirror or, better, a collection of prisms that reflect and refract reality. By showing us its various interpretations (perhaps the husband really loved his wife, was lost without her, and hence felt he must kill himself; perhaps she really thought to save her husband by a show of affection for the bandit, and thus played the role of faithful wife; perhaps the woodcutter knows much more, perhaps he too entered the action—mirrors within mirrors, each intention bringing forth another, until the triangle fades into the distance) he has shown first that human beings are incapable of judging reality, much less truth, and, second, that they must continually deceive themselves if they are to remain true to the ideas of themselves that they have.

Here then, more than in any other single film, is found Kurosawa's central theme: the world is illusion, you yourself make reality, but this reality undoes you if you submit to being limited by what you have made. The important corollary—you are not, however, truly subject to this reality, you can break free from it, can live even closer to the nature you are continually creating—this occurs only in the later films.

Production

The visual starting point remains the Akutagawa stories. The author's description of the gate and medieval Kyoto is literally followed by both the script and camera. . . . What turned out to be an excellent cinematic device, all the testimonies being given to the audience, questions answered by unheard questions being repeated as a question and then answered by those testifying, is taken directly from the author. Likewise, in the original script, all the characters' names are retained even though, in the case of hus-

Kurosawa on location. (Courtesy of University of California Press.)

band and wife, they never appear in the dialogue. Given the eventual difference between story and film—which is extreme and which the Japanese critics complained of when they said the director had been false to the spirit of the tales—such literal fidelity is remarkable.

The acting style, however, owes nothing at all to Akutagawa or any of his suggestions. It springs from a different source. "We were staying in Kyoto," says Kurosawa, "waiting for the sets to be finished. While we were waiting there we ran off some 16 mm. prints to amuse ourselves. One of them was a Martin Johnson jungle film in which there was a shot of a lion roaming around. I noticed it and told Mifune [the bandit] that that was just what I wanted him to be. At the same time Mori [the samurai] had seen a jungle picture in which a black leopard was shown. We all went to see it. When the leopard came on Machiko [the wife] was so upset that she hid her face. I saw and recognized the gesture. It was just what I wanted for the young wife."

Cinematically the style is made of various parts, all of which work admirably together. Perhaps the most noticeable is a kind of rhapsodic impressionism which from time to time carries the story and creates the atmosphere. Take, for example, the much-admired walk of the woodcutter through the forest. This is pure cinema impressionism—one literally receives impressions: the passing trees overhead, the sun, the glint of sunlight on the ax. Again, during the rape scene, the camera seeks the sky, the sun, the trees, contrasting this with the two, wife and bandit. When the rape is consummated and just before we return to the prison courtyard for the conclusion of the bandit's story, the sun comes out from behind a branch, dazzling, shining directly into the lenses: a metaphor. Just as much a metaphor certainly as the scene shortly before where she drops her dagger and it falls point first to land upright, quivering in the ground; or the celebrated scene where Mifune is asleep and the two pass. He has mentioned the breeze in his testimony. Now we see it (accompanied by the cooling celesta on the sound track) as it ruffles his hair. He opens his eyes and sees it raising her veil. It is an extended metaphor, a two-line poem. In Kurosawa's later films, this impressionism is not often seen, though there is a fine example at the end of *Sanjuro* where, after all the camellias have been sent off down the stream, there is a pause and then, as the bad man falls, a single blossom falls all by itself, and is carried away—the perfect classic metaphor for the cut-short life.

Kurosawa in this film, and more than in any other, makes use of contrasting shots. A shot of the woman is held for a certain length of time. This is matched by a shot of the bandit, held for the same time. He intercuts these, back and forth, matching the timing so delicately that one does not notice the number of repeats while watching the film—and is surprised upon reading the script to discover that there are so many.

In the same way he uses single close-ups to emphasize the triangular nature of the story. A shot of the woman is followed by a shot of the bandit is followed by a shot of the husband, and this process continues, going round and round as it were. Mostly, however, he insists upon the triangle through composition. The picture is filled with masterful triangular compositions, often one following directly after another, the frame filled with woman, bandit, husband, but always in different compositional relationships to each other. When the Japanese critics mentioned Kurosawa's "silent-film technique" they meant his great reliance upon composition—which with this film became, and still remains, one of the strongest elements of his film style.

Kurosawa's use of cinematic punctuation is always imaginative and, as we have seen, he is one of the few directors remaining who can intelligently use that most maligned of punctuation marks: the wipe. There is a fine use of it when the woman is waiting, during the bandit's story, and it (as always with Kurosawa) gives the effect of time, usually a short period of time, having elapsed. Here, as in *Ikiru,* the wipe is masterfully used. In *The Idiot,* on the other hand, Kurosawa was so unsure (because he was filming his favorite novel, by his favorite author, and doing it for a then-uncooperative company) that he used the wipe within a single scene, not once but many times, and the time indicated as having passed can only be a matter of seconds. . . .

Kurosawa does not usually use fades (either in or out) tending to be suspicious of the softening effect they produce. Certainly the ending of *The Lower Depths*—it ends on an unexpected cut—would be far less effective with a fade-out. He uses it only, as in the opening and closing of *The Throne of Blood,* when he deliberately wants the effect of distance and uninvolvement. For Kurosawa the fade usually means the elegiac.

The dissolve on the other hand usually means time passing. The end of *Rashomon* is a beautiful example of this. The three men are standing under the gate and there is a series of dissolves moving closer and closer. This is almost a rhetorical device since, in actuality, not much time could have passed. It is a formal gesture, a gesture which makes us look, and makes us feel. If the purpose is merely to indicate passage of time, however, Kurosawa has even simpler ways of doing it—one of the most imaginative in this picture is where the husband is waiting and his voice tells us that he waited a very long time. Here the effect is given through three shots [shots 292–294] with no dissolves or wipes at all—simply a long shot, followed by a medium shot, followed by a close-up. These are used so consummately that one does not question that hours have passed.

Kurosawa's preoccupation with time (*the* preoccupation for any serious director) began with *Rashomon.* There are two kinds of time which concern him—and any other director. One is ostensible time—the time the story takes. The other is a certain kind of psychological time, the time that each sequence, and that each shot within this sequence, takes. The first kind is the kind which is appreciable to the audience as well. *Rashomon* is a series of flashbacks, all of them both true and false. . . .

The second kind of time is the kind of which no audience is aware—this is created in the alchemy of the cutting room, and it is telling that Kurosawa takes almost as long to cut as he does to shoot a film.

In *Rashomon* one remembers a series of seemingly actual, or at least realistic, actions. And yet the film—

extraordinarily so, even for Kurosawa—is a mosaic. The average of the shorter shots is 2 feet (1⅓ seconds) and, though there are several shorter shots, and though shots also last for a minute or more (the dialogue scenes under the gate), still, the average length of each shot is shorter in *Rashomon* than in any other of Kurosawa's films. This always has the effect of reality on the screen. As Naoki Noborikawa has noticed: "In *Rashomon* there is a scene where Tajomaru takes Takehiro [the husband] into the woods, then runs back and tells the woman that her husband has been bitten by a snake. The scenery through which the two together run to where he has left the husband tied up is full of great natural beauty, but the camera passes by it in one flash. I had thought that this was one shot, a swiftly moving pan. Seeing the film for the second time, however, I noticed that this was not so, and when I counted, on seeing it for the third time, I was surprised to discover that there were [four] cuts in this small scene." [See shots 133–136.] As Kurosawa knew full well, one cuts fast and often for fast sections, slow and seldom for slow. But another reason for the extreme brevity of the *Rashomon* shots might be that the director knew he was asking his audience to look at the same material four or more times. He could not rely upon the novelty of the pictorial image to help sustain interest.

In addition, and maybe for the same reasons, he probably never moved the camera more than in *Rashomon*. The shooting script is full of directions to pan, to dolly in and out, etc. He used a favorite device of a dolly shot directly attached to a pan shot to get a continuity of action, and he was unusually careful of action continuity. This great mobility never calls attention to itself but gives the effect of continuous movement which we remember as being part of the style of the film.

All of these shots, stationary or moving, are superbly

calculated as to their time on the screen and their effect there. There are few other directors who know so precisely the proper length for a given section of film. The shot of the dog carrying the human hand at the opening of *Yojimbo* is an example. One second less and we would not have known what he was carrying; one second more and the scene would have been forced, vulgar. In *Rashomon* the dagger drops into the ground and is allowed to quiver not often but just twice. All of the images are handled in this imaginative and economical manner.

Kurosawa rarely makes a mistake in his timing, and the inner or psychological timing of *Rashomon* is perfection. There are 407 separate shots in the body of the film (with about 12 more for titles). This is more than twice the number in the usual film, and yet these shots never call attention to themselves—rather, they make it possible for us to feel this film, to be reached with immediacy, to be drawn into it, intellectually curious and emotionally aware. In a very special way, *Rashomon*—like any truly fine film—creates within its audience the very demand which it satisfies.

For a director as young as Kurosawa—he was then forty—and particularly for so young a Japanese director, the film is remarkably free from influences. Though some scenes owe much to Dovzhenko's *Aerograd,* they owe nothing at all to Fritz Lang's *Siegfried* (an ostensible "influence" often mentioned) because the director has never seen it. The structure may owe something to *The Marriage Circle,* that Lubitsch film which Kurosawa—like most Japanese directors—remembers with affection and admiration, but the debt is very slight.

Of the style, Kurosawa has said only: "I like silent pictures and I always have. They are often so much more beautiful than sound pictures are. Perhaps they had to be. At any rate, I wanted to restore some of this beauty. I thought of it, I remember, in this way:

one of the techniques of modern art is simplification, and that I must therefore simplify this film." Simplification is also one of the techniques of Japanese art and long has been. Those who noticed a "Japanese" look about some of the scenes (mainly their composition, aside from temple architecture, sand gardens, and the like) were right, though the director had perhaps reached this through his own knowledge of simplified painting techniques in the West—those of Klee and Matisse, for example. Otherwise there is little "Japanese" influence. In fact the film is the complete opposite of the ordinary Japanese historical film in that it questions while they reaffirm; it is completely realistic while they are always romantic; it is using its period as a pretext and a decoration while the ordinary period film aims at simple reconstruction. Despite foreign commentators on the subject, there is absolutely no influence at all from classical Japanese drama. Only the sword-fighting techniques owe something to the modern Japanese stage. Anyone who has ever seen Kabuki will realize the enormous difference between its acting style and that of *Rashomon*. The acting in the film is naturalistic, in the Japanese sense of the word. It is apparently unrestrained, and it is in the grand manner which the West once knew but has now almost lost. Indeed, Mifune as the bandit was so "grand" that even Japanese critics complained of overacting. There is another debt to the stage, however, though the stage is Japanese modern theater—the Shingeki. Since the budget was small the sets (there are only two—both studio sets—the gate and the prison courtyard) are deliberately stylized, deliberately simplified in the manner of modern stage scenery (again, not Kabuki scenery, which is flamboyant, detailed, and very nineteenth century to the eye). Likewise, the costumes owe much to modern stage costumes, with their simplicity, their lack of ornament. Too—the music owes much to incidental-music methods on the modern Japanese stage. That the music owes even more to another source is so notorious some critics (Western) have admitted the film was partially spoiled for them. This is not the fault of the composer. The late Fumio Hayasaka was one of Japan's most individual and creative composers and it was Kurosawa himself who said "write something like Ravel's *Boléro*"—a work which in Japan had not yet become as clichéd as in the West. The composer complied and the results, as a matter of fact, do detract—particularly from the opening scenes. . . .

The shooting time for the film was unusually short

When Daiei photographed the publicity stills for Rashomon, *they asked the cast to mug and clown for many of the shots* (see above). *Daiei apparently believed that comic stills would help explain the purpose of what they felt was an unaccountably "exaggerated" acting style in the film. During the same publicity session, other photos were taken (the ones ultimately released), which stressed the "glamor-adventure" side of the movie. (See pp. 236–37. The girl in the bathing suit is Machiko Kyo, who plays the wife. The photo was sent out as part of the* Rashomon *publicity.)*

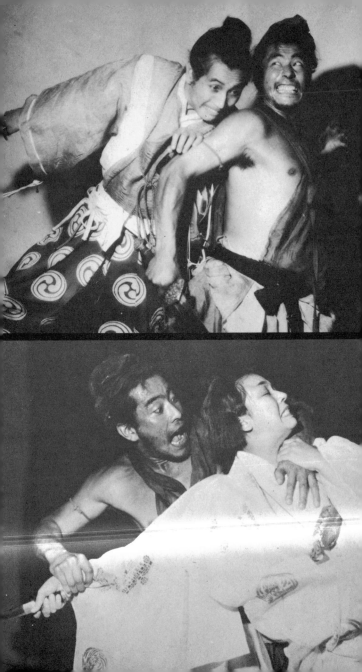

(it was completed within a matter of weeks because most of the pre-production work had been done for some time) and is one of the few Kurosawa pictures that did not go over budget. Daiei did release it with some care. It was given a formal premiere in what was then one of Tokyo's best theaters; the press was invited and it was given an initial run of two weeks (even now the usual run is only a single week) at all the theaters in the Daiei chain. Contrary to later legend, it was not a box office failure—it ranked fourth in Daiei's listing of best money-earners in the 1950's. Nor did the audience seem to have trouble understanding it—though occasionally an apprehensive theater manager would hire a *benshi,* a lecturer-commentator, to talk throughout the film, hinting what it was about.

Daiei, though more pleased than not with its second Kurosawa picture, made no attempt to detain him when he returned to Toho, and after the second and third runs were completed, shelved the picture. There it would probably have remained to this day had it not been for a series of fortuitous circumstances which led to its becoming the best-known Japanese film ever made.

Venice sent an invitation to Japan asking that a film be entered in the film festival. This was before Japan became as well-acquainted with film festivals as it is now, and there was consternation as to what to send. *Rashomon* was not even considered. In the meantime, at the request of Venice, Guilliana Stramigioli, then head of Italiafilm in Japan, had viewed a number of Japanese films, had seen *Rashomon,* and had liked it. When she recommended it, however, the suggestion was met with much opposition—particularly from Daiei, which had neither hope for nor faith in the film. It was with the greatest reluctance that they agreed to sending the film to the 1951 Venice Festival, where it won first prize.

Its winning what was then the best-thought-of cinema prize came as a profound shock to Japan. For one thing, it had not been made for export, and there remains a long-standing Japanese prejudice that things not especially constructed for foreigners will not be understood by them. For another, the Japanese critics had not liked the film. Tadashi Iijima thought the film failed because of "its insufficient plan for visualizing the style of the original stories"; Tatsuhiko Shigeno objected to the language, saying that no robber would ever use words that big. Other critics thought the script was too complicated, or that the direction was too monotonous, or that there was too much rough language.

What perhaps most surprised the Japanese, however, was that a historical film (and they continued to think of *Rashomon* as "historical" in the "costume-picture" sense of the word) should prove acceptable to the West. This eventually led to a rash of Western-aimed "historical" films—of which *Gate of Hell* is the only surviving example—but initially critics were at a loss to explain its winning the Venice prize and its consequent popularity in most other countries. Eventually, they decided that it was because *Rashomon* was "exotic" (in the sense that *Gate of Hell* is truly exotic —and little else) and that foreigners like exoticism. Even now it is the rare critic who will admit that *Rashomon* could have had any other appeal to the West.

Once the rare critic is found, however, he will say— as several have—that the reason the West liked it was because the reasoning in the picture was "Western," by which is meant analytic, logical, and speculative. . . . Actually, of course, what had happened is that in this film (though not for the first time in Japanese cinema history) the confines of "Japanese" thought could not contain the director who thereby joined the world at large. *Rashomon* speaks to everyone, not just to the Japanese.

Kurosawa has said: "The Japanese are terribly critical of Japanese films, so it is not too surprising that a foreigner should have been responsible for my film's being sent to Venice. It was the same way with Japanese woodcuts—it was the foreigners who first appreciated them. We Japanese think too little of our own things. Actually, *Rashomon* wasn't all that good, I don't think. Yet, when people have said to me that its reception was just a stroke of luck, a fluke, I have answered by saying that they only say these things because the film is, after all, Japanese, and then I wonder: Why do we all think so little of our own things? Why don't we stand up for our films? What are we so afraid of?"

Though Daiei did not retain the director, it followed the usual maxim of film companies: if you have a success, repeat it. In the following year Daiei's Keigo Kimura made *The Beauty and the Bandits* which was taken directly from *Rashomon,* and the much better *Tale of Genji* by Kimisaburo Yoshimura. Kurosawa himself, his reputation enormously enhanced by the international success of the film, went back to Toho to make *Ikiru.* Show-biz decided that Japan had made an unexampled breakthrough into the "foreign market," and the man on the street was as delighted over the Venice prize as he would have been had a Japanese athlete won an Olympics medal. Thus, in a way, the worth of *Rashomon* was partially obscured by its own success. It was only much later that one could realize that it is one of the few living films from Japan's cinematic past. Its frequent revivals in Japan, its frequent re-showings in other countries, its constant appearance in retrospectives, the fact that it is still talked about, still discussed, makes one finally realize that, along with *Ikiru* and *Seven Samurai,* it is a masterpiece.

Adaptation of Rashomon

All stills from the M-G-M release The Outrage. *Howard Da Silva plays the prospector; Edward G. Robinson, the con man; and William Shatner, the preacher.*

The Outrage

An Excerpt from the Screenplay
by Michael Kanin

1 *Lightning and a crash of thunder introduce the main title, seen against a dark foreboding sky, at the height of a violent rainstorm.*

As each new credit title appears, it is accompanied by further crashes and rumblings of thunder, lightning flashes, howls of the wind, and sudden gusts of rain.

After the titles, camera (from its high angle) moves forward. Slowly, through the dusk, through the mist and the rain, a smallish "whistle-stop" railroad station begins to appear dimly. As we approach it, another flash of lightning briefly illumines the glistening train tracks disappearing far off somewhere.

The station itself (when camera finally holds it in a full shot) gives evidences of having been a busy, bustling place at one time. But now, deserted, ramshackle, it huddles wet and gray and forlorn in the downpour, and seems to reflect the physical and spiritual decay of its locality. The wooden boards of the main platform are warped and toothless in spots; the sagging portico over it provides little protection against the rain. A rusty sign, barely legible, still has the pretentiously-lettered name of the town on it: "SILVER GULCH." What used to be the ticket booth and waiting room are now dark and empty, the wind whistling through their broken windows. A hand truck lies overturned on one

The Outrage © 1964 Metro-Goldwyn-Mayer Inc. and KHF Productions. Excerpt from the screenplay by Michael Kanin furnished through the courtesy of Metro-Goldwyn-Mayer Inc., distributors of the Martin Ritt Production *The Outrage* starring Paul Newman, Laurence Harvey, Claire Bloom, Edward G. Robinson, William Shatner, Howard Da Silva, Albert Salmi, produced by A. Ronald Lubin and directed by Martin Ritt.

end of the platform, which is dotted with the white droppings of crows and with rank grass growing in the crevices.

In one of the few dry spots on the platform, a preacher sits on an old bench. Beside him is a threadbare carpet satchel and a few clumsily wrapped bundles—all his worldly possessions.

2 *Close shot, the preacher.* He seems much more tired and haggard than his thirty-odd years warrant—a study in defeat—as he holds his frayed coat closely about him and stares sadly off into space.

3 *Exterior. A dirt road, dusk.* It is rutted, muddy, full of weeds. A grizzled prospector is slogging along hurriedly through the rain, dragging his burro behind him. The bedraggled animal is laden down with customary tools and paraphernalia. The prospector, equally bedraggled, is one of the many who have never struck it rich—a simple soul who doggedly tries to eke out a meager living in the only way he knows. In the distance, in the direction from which he's coming, can be seen the starkly etched silhouette of a town.

4 *Another angle. The prospector is going toward the railroad station, not far ahead of him.*

5 *Close shot, the prospector. He stops momentarily, wipes the rain off his face and peers forward as if looking for someone. Then, with a jerk at his burro's head, he moves on again.*

6 *Ext. The railroad station, dusk. Out of breath, the prospector approaches the rear of the station. There's a certain eeriness about this place that makes him wary. He looks through an open doorway into the shadowy waiting room and shoves his burro inside, out of the rain. Camera follows him as, looking this way and that, he moves around toward the front of the station, where the platform parallels the tracks.*

7 *Another angle. Coming around from the rear, the prospector stops short at the sight of the preacher sitting alone at the other end of the platform. Not very articulate at best, he seems particularly moved by the obvious fact of the preacher's departure, and just stands there, trying to find the words to express himself. The preacher looks up, vaguely recognizes him, and turns away again. The prospector shuffles over to him, very respectful and deferential, suddenly feeling self-conscious about his grimy, disreputable appearance. The least he can do, he thinks, is take off his hat.*

PROSPECTOR: 'Scuse me, Preacher—I mean, fer buttin' in. I jest couldn't believe it down to the general store when they sez, "The preacher's up an' left us." I sez, "He wouldn't do nothin' like that. Wait an' see, he'll be back sure." (*He looks at the preacher's satchel and bundles.*) But then I . . . warn't sure—

The preacher turns his head away. The prospector wipes his face, profoundly perplexed.

PROSPECTOR: [I know—it was like a nightmare,]* what we seed an' heerd at the trial yesterday. My skin's been a-creepin' ever since. Didn't make no sense, no sense at all. (*Earnestly.*) But . . . you leavin' the church—your place here, the people who need you—that don't make no sense neither.

[PREACHER: What does make sense?

PROSPECTOR: Doggoned if I know, sir. I ain't got no more brains than my donkey. Else, I wouldn't o' gone scratchin' around in the earth all these years, tryin' t' strike it rich. But—]

He stops as a flash of lightning is followed by a crack of thunder. The preacher rises and steps forward, looking up at the dark clouds and letting the rain pelt his face.

PREACHER: I can understand the violence of a storm. [It's a natural thing—not meant to harm anyone.]

8 *Close-up, preacher. If we didn't know it was rain running down his face in rivulets, it might look like tears.*

PREACHER: But the violence of men—their cruelty and savageness to one another—and to themselves—

9 *Full shot. The prospector gently draws the preacher back out of the rain.*

PROSPECTOR: Please—you'll catch yer death.

The preacher moves to the other end of the platform, peering through the rain along the receding ribbon of tracks. The prospector shuffles up behind him.

PROSPECTOR: That train ain't gonna be along for

---

* The final dialogue of the film was somewhat different at certain points. We have bracketed the major omissions and footnoted the altered speeches here and elsewhere. In the final film, this phrase was: "It didn't make sense at all . . ."
—*Eds.*

hours. Hardly ever stops here these days. I'll flag it down fer you when it comes. (*Solicitously.*) Here—lemme make us a fire.

During the following, he proceeds to collect some splinters of wood and to light up a meager, sputtering bonfire in a spot where a few boards of the platform are missing. The preacher moves around the station platform, sensing acutely the air of disintegration about it. The station sign looms up before him, dangling askew in the wind.

PREACHER: Silver Gulch! I remember when I first came here. I was going to strike it rich, too. A bonanza of souls to save! (*Ironically.*) "I will lead them in paths that they have not known, I will make darkness light before them—and crooked things straight."

He reaches up to straighten the sign. It falls to the ground and is splattered with mud. He looks down at it, as if seeing his dashed hopes symbolized.

PROSPECTOR: Ev'rybody sez—when you git yer steam up, you do some powerful preachifyin'.

PREACHER: Yes—to a congregation of deaf ears. (*Turning.*) And the ones at the trial yesterday. You heard it all. (*Bitterly.*) Christians!

PROSPECTOR: Jest can't understand it. All that sinnin'
—lustin' and killin'. An' then in front o' the judge,
swearin' on the Holy Bible to tell the whole truth an'
—the way they— (*Shaking his head.*) There must be
some answer, but I'm too ignorant to explain it.

PREACHER: Not as ignorant as *I* am.

PROSPECTOR (*shocked*): No, Preacher, no. You're
eddicated—you're a man o' God—

*There's a distant, angry roll of thunder. The prospector
looks up, shifting uneasily from one foot to the other.*

PREACHER: Yes—*He* knows. He knows I've failed Him.
(*With a heavy sigh.*) The shepherd is running away
from the wolves.

[PROSPECTOR (*weakly*): Don't say that—please—

PREACHER: Faith requires a strong stomach.]

*There's a pause as the prospector stares at him, at a
loss.*

PROSPECTOR: Where d'ya aim t' be goin'?

PREACHER: I don't know—I don't know—

VOICE: How about going plumb to hell!

*The preacher and the prospector look around, startled,
as the con man appears in an open doorway, scratching himself sleepily and muttering.*

CON MAN: Fella can't sleep in peace around this
horseball of a town!

Despite his dishevelled, seedy appearance, he's clearly not a common tramp. The gray derby with the sharply curved brim, the cravat, the spats, though threadbare and mud-spattered at the moment, all suggest that he originated in some large Eastern city, and that his career has been as checkered as his vest. For most of his many years, he has used every conceivable swindle, bunco racket, and confidence game in his pursuit of the easy buck. It's hard to believe that he was ever, even at birth, anything but a cynic.

PROSPECTOR (*recognizing him*): Oh, it's you! Didn't figger you'd have the guts t' show up 'round these parts again.

CON MAN (*eyeing him sourly*): I never forget a face, my good man. But I'm glad to make an exception in your case.

Inside the waiting room, the prospector's burro has come up behind the vagrant. Now, suddenly, it brays loudly. The con man leaps out onto the platform with an exclamation of surprise. Wheeling around, he sees the burro in the doorway. It brays again.

CON MAN (*riled*): Hee-haw up your tail, you Godforsaken jackass!

PROSPECTOR: Shet up, you! This is a *preacher* settin' here.

CON MAN: Preacher? (*Gives the preacher an appraising glance.*) Can't be. He woke me up. They usually put me to sleep.

PROSPECTOR (*to the preacher, protectively*): Don't pay 'im no mind.

PREACHER: Who is he?

PROSPECTOR: He's a con man, a swindler—an old scalawag!

CON MAN: How *else* can you live to be old nowadays?

Seeing the fire, he crouches beside it to warm himself, increasing the flames with odds and ends of debris.

PROSPECTOR (*to preacher*): He come 'round last year, sellin' some kind o' patent medicine—

CON MAN (*grandiloquently*): Choctaw Herbal Elixir!

PROSPECTOR: Three people near died from it. He got out o' town jest ahead o' the tar an' feathers.

CON MAN (*amused*): [And there I was again this morning, trying to sell lightning rods to the same old suckers. (*He laughs.*) What a boner!]*

---

* In the final film, this speech was: "So you can imagine my surprise this morning when I realized where the devil I was. I'd just sold a dozen of my fully guaranteed miracle lightning rods to the same old suckers. Then, all of a sudden, it started thundering and lightning like there was a heavenly inspector testing the guarantees."

PROSPECTOR: You're lower'n a rattler!

CON MAN: Oh, come now, my cantankerous friend, we're not so different, you and me. I dig for silver, too, only in much softer ground. (*Pause.*) Though, I must say, this town of yours has sure gone to pot. What happened? The silver peter out? It's a sure sign, when the whores and gamblers start heading for the next sucker town.

PROSPECTOR: Good riddance.

CON MAN (*to preacher*): Nothing much left to preach about, eh, Reverend? Ah, but I forgot—*you're* leaving, too. Had a bellyful of religion, I take it. (*Snaps fingers.*) Say how about the two of us teaming up? We could make a hatful—with your face an' my fingers.

The preacher rises and moves away.

PROSPECTOR: Leave 'im be!

CON MAN (*in mock innocence*): Just said he's got an honest face. What's wrong with that?

The prospector takes a few steps toward the preacher, but doesn't quite know how to comfort him.

PROSPECTOR: He's as rotten as those three at the trial yesterday.

CON MAN: Trial? What trial? (*They don't answer.*) Something happen around here?

PROSPECTOR (*after a pause, grudgingly*): A man was murdered.

CON MAN: Just *one*? A slow day.

The prospector shivers and draws his damp clothes more tightly around him. After a moment's hesitation, he shuffles over to the fire and warms his hands, as the con man fans the feeble flames.

CON MAN (*looks up at him*): You look green around the gills. 'Smatter, you lettin' a little murder upset your tummy?

PROSPECTOR: It warn't the murder itself. It was— (*He stops.*)

CON MAN: It was what . . . what?

PROSPECTOR: The way it happened—the things we heerd at the trial—

CON MAN (*thumbing the preacher*): What'd *he* have to do with it?

PROSPECTOR: We was subpoeneed, both of us.

CON MAN: Why?

PROSPECTOR: I was the one found the body.

CON MAN (*intrigued*): Yeah? Where?

PROSPECTOR: In the woods—a few miles west o' town—

10 *Ext. Scenic panorama, long shot, day. The sun is high and hot. In the distance, coming from a wide stretch of desert prairie, the prospector is leading his*

burro up into the foothills of a mountain range. Wearily, they cut across the ruts of a wagon trail and trudge up the incline toward the wooded higher ground.

PROSPECTOR'S VOICE: Days like that, when it gits too hot at the diggin's, I head for a ravine I know, where I kin soak a bit in a pool underneath the falls.

[11 *Back at the railroad station. Close-up, the con man.*]

CON MAN (*impatiently*): Never mind that. What about the body?

12 *Ext. The foothills, day. Moving behind the prospector and his burro as they stamp their way through a thicket.*

PROSPECTOR'S VOICE: I didn't see it—I mean, not right off.*

13 *Moving shot, through the thicket (prospector's point of view, his shadow flickering on the undergrowth ahead).*

[PROSPECTOR'S VOICE (*continued*): First, I come across this trampled spot—]

Camera slows cautiously as the flattened piece of thicket comes into view.

[PROSPECTOR'S VOICE: Thought mebbe it were a bear or somethin'.]

14 *Close, the burro's pack. The prospector's hand takes a rifle out of a saddle holster.*

---

* In the final film, the prospector's three subsequent speeches are replaced by the following continuation of his speech here in shot 12: "But I don't know, there was something about the way the air hung heavy all around (*the camera is panning as he passes behind huge cacti*)—even the woods. It gave me a kind o' nervous, prickly feelin'."

15 *Moving shot, through the thicket.*

[PROSPECTOR'S VOICE: Then I see the hat, the straw
   hat with the veil on it—]

*Camera slows again as the hat is suddenly there on the
ground. The prospector's hand reaches into the shot
and picks it up.*

[PROSPECTOR'S VOICE: It give me a kind o' shiver,
   seein' as how it warn't no likely place fer a woman.]

M-G-M publicity still showing the first encounter between the bandit, Juan Carrasco (Paul Newman), and the husband and wife (Laurence Harvey and Claire Bloom, respectively).

The play Rashomon, by Fay and Michael Kanin, opened on Broadway January 27, 1959, with a cast headed by Rod Steiger and Claire Bloom. Noel Willman played the husband; Akim Tamiroff, the woodcutter (= prospector); Oscar Homolka, the wigmaker (= commoner or con man); and Michael Shillo, the priest (= preacher). Peter Glenville directed, David Susskind and Hardy Smith co-produced.